ALWAYS CHEAT

The Philosophy of Jesse Ventura

Leslie Davis

Library of Congress Control Number: 2002091247

ISBN 0-9719261-0-7

Copyright 2002 Tell The Truth Books, Inc.

Tell The Truth Books, Inc.
P.O. Box 11688
Minneapolis, MN 55411
www.lesliedavis.com

All cartoon and cover art by Pete Wagner
www.wagtoons.com

Art direction by Chank
www.chank.com

Edited by Chemistry Creative

Text and cover printed on recycled paper.
Text is 100% post-consumer recycled paper.

Printed in Minnesota, USA

Table of Contents

ALWAYS CHEAT

Acknowledgements

Jenny K. Aylward
Chank
Cursor.org
William Dahn
Linda Das
Henry Fieldseth
Dick Franson
Carol Kellogg
Steve Kimmel
Lynn Levine
Colleen Meyer
Kathy Norris
Keith Reitman
Gabriel Rios
Bill Salisbury
Ole Savior
Pete Wagner
Chris Wright

Biography

Pete Wagner

Pete Wagner is a political cartoonist and activist.

Wagner's cartoons have won seven national and regional awards, including the Society of Professional Journalists and Minnesota Public Interest Research Group Public Citizen Award.

His 27 years as a controversial cartoonist include 10 as staff editorial cartoonist for *City Pages,* the major alternative weekly newspaper of Minneapolis, Minnesota, seven with the *Minnesota Daily* in Minneapolis and one year with the *Madison* (Wisconsin) *Press Connection*—a Daily, organized and run entirely by its employees as a co-op rather than a corporation. In the late 1970s, Wagner was hired by Larry Flynt to do a regular political cartoon for *Hustler* Magazine.

Wagner's cartoons have been syndicated and reprinted in more than 300 newspapers and magazines, including; *In These Times,* the *Progressive, High Times, New Age Journal, Z, Time* Magazine, *The Washington Post, Chicago Sun Times, Milwaukee Journal, Minneapolis Star Tribune, St. Paul Pioneer Press* and *St. Louis Post-Dispatch* and they were exhibited in the Whitney Museum.

As an activist, Wagner has used humor to myth-make and organize. While attending the University of Minnesota, he ran for student president on the "Tupperware Party" ticket and he defeated 11 other candidates in the primary. He later organized the Brain Trust street theater troupe, which published a political art magazine and organized events like the Generic (All-Purpose) Demonstration, attracting over 5000 participants who demonstrated for or against anything they wanted.

To see Wagner's extensive work, please go to www.wagtoons.com.

Preface

Always Cheat reveals how Jesse Ventura and his campaign chairman Dean Barkley, bribed and induced a registered candidate to withdraw from the Reform Party.

They had two reasons for their illegal act: one was so Ventura could keep his radio talk show and the other was to remove Ventura's competition in the September 1998 Reform Party primary election.

Ventura and Barkley also "fixed" and "controlled" the subsequent investigation.

Ventura, Barkley and the people they bribed, all violated Minnesota Statute 211B.10, Subdivision 1.

> **"A person may not reward or promise to reward another in any manner to induce the person to be or refrain from or cease being a candidate. A person may not solicit or receive a payment, promise, or reward from another for this purpose."**

Always Cheat is factually supported with recorded investigative interviews, transcripts, voice mail messages, video recordings, government memos, news articles, letters and personal interviews.

Always Cheat explains how Governor Ventura removed from their jobs those Minnesota state employees who objected to his illegal activities—such as the job he accepted as a wrestling referee in August 1999.

Always Cheat confirms that Ventura was not a U.S. Navy SEAL while on active duty, as he has claimed on several occasions. It also confirms that Ventura was never engaged in combat, another of his false claims.

Always Cheat lists dozens of Ventura quotes that verbally abuse groups of people.

Author's Message

Leslie Davis

www.LeslieDavis.com

U.S. Army veteran – Businessman
Environmental activist – Political candidate

Steve Kimmel - Leslie Davis - Linda Das
on the campaign trail, Duluth, Minnesota, 1998

Has anyone ever told you—*hey, you should write a book!*
Well, a number of people have told me that I should
write a book about Minnesota Governor Jesse Ventura.

So I did. This is it.

Always Cheat is a no holds barred book about Jesse Ventura's antics since July 1998.

Since 1983, as the founder and president of the Earth Protector environmental group, I have been intimately involved in numerous environmental, social justice and political issues.

Leslie Davis and Ventura effigy in front of Minneapolis City Hall opposing the light rail location. – *Minnesota 2000*

Earth Protector is dedicated to protecting the environment and public health.

We assist individuals and communities confronting pollution problems, review pollution permits proposed by government agencies, educate in the schools and promote hydrogen fuel, fuel cells and organic sustainable agriculture.

In 1998, I ran for governor against Jesse Ventura in order to offer sensible solutions to Minnesota's incorrect energy, environmental, economic, education and public health policies. I shared many of my views with Ventura and I found him to be congenial and open. I thought he had a good chance of winning.

On the night Ventura won, my friends and I went to his victory party to congratulate him and celebrate. When he saw me in the crowd he came over to shake my hand and say, "we won." I took that literally, so I sent him a check for his transition team, a T-shirt from my Earth Protector environmental group and my credentials offering to help him be a great governor, with or without compensation.

I was an early ardent supporter of Jesse Ventura, but was disappointed when he did and said cruel and dishonest things that you will read about throughout *Always Cheat.*

Everything in **Always Cheat** is supported by sworn affidavits, transcripts, voice mails, taped investigative interviews, videos, memorandums, newspaper articles, letters and personal interviews.

Ventura may try to discredit this book by saying that I:

- **Never liked him**
- **Am angry because he won the election**
- **Have been trying to damage him since he won the election**

    ALL THREE STATEMENTS ARE FALSE

On November 5, 1998, two days after Ventura's election, I sent him a letter offering my support and challenging him to "Dare to be Great." Like all Minnesotans, I wish he had been up to the challenge.

I received several letters from Steven Bosacker, Ventura's chief of staff for the transition team, who later became chief of staff for the administration. One Bosacker letter dated December 11, 1998, thanked me for offering my help and acknowledged receipt of my credentials.

On December 30, 1998, I sent Ventura a letter withdrawing my support and requested removal of my name from consideration for any position in the Ventura administration.

Bosacker sent me a letter on January 27, 1999, acknowledging the withdrawal of my support.

All four letters are reproduced on the following pages for the purpose of documenting my early commitment to help Ventura.

Davis for Governor

622 Lowry Avenue North
Minneapolis, MN 55411-1441
612/522-9433
FAX 612/521-5506
e-mail Davisgov@aol.com
http://members.aol.com/davisgov/index.html

November 5, 1998   **Total FAX is 2 pages**

Dear Jesse,

                    "Dare To Be Great"

My heartfelt congratulations to you and your helpers. You did
what I know could be done. That's why I ran twice.

I would like to help your transition team and your
administration. With or without money.

My areas of expertise are environment (electricity conservation,
renewable energy, fuel cells, wind and hydrogen), health (lead
poisoning, asthma and cancer), industrial fiber/hemp and the
economy. I would be well-suited in the economic/environmental/
industrial/development area.

Before Earth Protector I was in manufacturing, marketing, trend
analysis and sales for 25 years as a six figure earner. I
attached one of my IRS income forms from 1979.

As the founder and president of Earth Protector, Inc. since 1982
I have been involved in activities before the Pollution Control
Agency, Department of Natural Resources, Department of Public
Service, Department of Agriculture, Metropolitan Council, U.S.
Forest Service, and many others. I have appeared before
innumerable city councils and county boards on behalf of Earth
Protector and the public. I am intimately familiar with their
activities.

Please call me anytime at 522-9433 to help you help the people.

Sincerely,

Leslie Davis

cc: Dean Barkley - FAX 479-6801

Attachment: 1979 IRS income form for Leslie Davis

P.S. By the way, T.V. Guide is a great publication to interview
      with. The Guide sits face up in front T.V.'s all week.

STATE OF MINNESOTA
OFFICE OF THE GOVERNOR-ELECT

JESSE VENTURA
GOVERNOR-ELECT

(651) 297-9500
ST. PAUL, MN 55155

ROOM B5
STATE CAPITOL

December 11, 1998

Ms. Leslie Davis
622 Lowry Ave. N.
Minneapolis, MN 55411-1441

Dear Ms. Davis:

Thank you for your interest in joining Governor-elect Ventura and Lieutenant Governor-elect Schunk in their new administration.

This letter acknowledges the receipt of your credentials.

Please be assured that every effort is being made to sort and organize the correspondence in a manner that will allow us to respond to all of you who are enthusiastically offering your support and indicating your interest in securing either an appointment or employment on the transition team or within the administration.

Again, we appreciate your interest. We will contact you directly if you are to be scheduled for an interview.

Sincerely,

Steven Bosacker

Steven Bosacker
Transition Chief of Staff

AN EQUAL OPPORTUNITY EMPLOYER

Earth Protector, Inc.

622 Lowry Avenue North
Minneapolis, Minnesota, USA 55411-1441
612/522-9433
FAX 612/521-5506
www.earthprotector.org

Protecting the Earth since 1983

December 30, 1998

Jesse Ventura
Room 85, State Capitol Building
St. Paul, Minnesota 55155

Dear Jesse:

The purpose of this letter is to express my contempt for your
actions the past several weeks and I hereby ask that you:
    ·remove my name from consideration for any position with
    your administration
    ·send back my transition team contribution
    ·return the Earth Protector T-shirt I sent you

Jesse, people who gun down animals released from cages at game
preserves are sick. (Pioneer Press December 8)

Knowing that you kill animals this way explains how you could
support and endorse the violent, terrorist and excessive force
raid conducted on a non-violent group of people ranging in age
from 14 to 72 at the Highway 55 site. (Star Tribune December 28)

There is overwhelming evidence that people who abuse animals
eventually abuse people and your actions have demonstrated the
accuracy of the evidence.

I was at the raid and saw every second of the action. Your
endorsement of that despicable raid brings disgrace upon you,
your family and your administration. The violent action against
peaceful people will be your legacy when we throw you out of
office in four years.

Several days after the raid I overheard a conversation to the
effect that when you were briefed on the raid you said that if
the people did not leave the houses they should be bulldozed
anyway. I can believe you would say something like that.

Jesse, from our short chats on the campaign trail and from your
warm handshake and greeting on victory night at Canterbury Downs
I had high hopes for you as Governor. That's all lost. The next
four years with you as Governor will be dark ones for Minnesota
but we will survive you as we did Carlson. Sad, sad, sad.

For the people, the animals and the environment,

Leslie Davis
President

       100% post consumer recycled paper without chlorine

STATE OF MINNESOTA

OFFICE OF GOVERNOR JESSE VENTURA
130 State Capitol • 75 Constitution Avenue • Saint Paul, MN 55155

January 27, 1999

Leslie Davis
Earth Protector, Inc.
622 Lowry Avenue North
Minneapolis, MN 55411

Dear Ms. Davis:

Pursuant to your request, enclosed is a check for $25.00 to reimburse you for your earlier contribution to Governor Ventura's transition. Also enclosed is your resume and t-shirt.

Sincerely,

Steven Bosacker

Steven Bosacker
Chief of Staff

SB/mh
Enclosures

Voice: (651) 296-3391 or (800) 657-3717 ◆ Fax: (651) 296-2089 ◆ TDD: (651) 296-0075 or (800) 657-3598
Web site: http://www.governor.state.mn.us   An Equal Opportunity Employer

Cast of Characters

Charles Balck, Ramsey County Assistant Attorney

Dean Barkley, Ventura Campaign Committee Chairman

Kathleen Blatz, Supreme Court Chief Justice

Steven Bosacker, Ventura's Chief of Staff

Karen Carpenter, Former Commissioner, Minnesota Department of Employee Relations

Julien C. Carter, Commissioner of Department of Employee Relations

Renee Coffey, Former Secretary of State staff person who registered Bill Dahn

Norm Coleman, Former Mayor of St. Paul and Republican gubernatorial candidate

William "Bill" Dahn, Candidate who was bribed by Ventura and Barkley

Leslie Davis, Author of this book

Diane Drewry, Ventura staff person and girlfriend of Ventura operative Phil Madsen

Henry Fieldseth, One of the people tortured during the Highway 55 raid

Tom Foley, Former Ramsey County Attorney that hired Susan Gaertner and John Wodele

Dick Franson, Army veteran who exposed Ventura military record and filed a complaint

Doug Friedline, Ventura Campaign Manager

Lynne Fundingsland, Acting Deputy, Minneapolis City Attorney's office

Susan Gaertner, Ramsey County Attorney

Kathleen Gearin, Ramsey County District Court Judge

Alan Gilbert, Chief Deputy, Minnesota Attorney General

Mike Hatch, Minnesota Attorney General. Alan Gilbert worked for him

Thomas Heffelfinger, U.S. Attorney and former attorney for Dean Barkley

Jay Heffern, Minneapolis City Attorney

Dennis Hoff, Ramsey County investigator

Hubert "Skip" Humphrey, Minn. Attorney General and DFL gubernatorial candidate

Mavis Huddle, Ventura's campaign secretary

Sandra Hyllengren, Former Ethics Officer with the Minn. Dept. of Employee Relations

James Kane, Bill Dahn's Lieutenant Governor

Amy Klobuchar, Hennepin County Attorney

Theodore D. Leon, Deputy City Attorney, City of St. Paul

Phil Madsen, Ventura operative, boyfriend of Diane Drewry

Joe Mansky, Elections Director with Secretary of State in July 1998

Teresa McFarland, Ventura transition spokeswoman

Gerald McNiff, Ramsey County investigator

James Molnar, Private investigator and Notary Public

Tim Penny, Former Congressman and Steven Bosacker friend

Jodene Pope, Former Secretary of State staff person in July 1998

Republican Party, Filed one of the original complaints about the Dahn bribe

Ole Savior, Candidate for Governor 1998

Bill Salisbury, Navy SEAL and Ventura critic

Mae Schunk, School teacher and Lieutenant Governor

Joe Soucheray, Newspaper columnist and radio talk show host

Tony Trimble, Attorney for Republican Party

Jesse Ventura, Governor of Minnesota

Phil Villaume, Attorney for Jesse Ventura and Dean Barkley

Charlie Weaver, Former prosecutor and legislator, now Commissioner of Public Safety

James Weber, Anoka County Prosecutor, Chief of the Criminal Division

John Wodele, Ventura's Communications Director

See detailed descriptions on Page 123

ALWAYS CHEAT

Chapter One

Jesse the Hero

It was November 1998 and Jesse "The Body" Ventura had just pulled off one of the most stunning political victories in United States history by winning the election for Governor of Minnesota. Who would have thought this former wrestler could become Minnesota's governor? It was a fantastic outcome for this seemingly comic book character.

Young and old, men and women, plenty of students and many first time voters showed up at the polls to show support for Ventura. They would not be denied their victory.

A total of 773,403 Minnesotans decided that Jesse Ventura the wrestler, actor, pseudo Navy SEAL and local hero would now manage almost five million people of the State of Minnesota.

I ran for governor in 1998 and Ventura and I chatted a few times on the campaign trail. One conversation was in August 1998 at a forum in St. Cloud, Minnesota. Ventura was haggard when he said, "I'm looking forward to going back to civilian life after the election."

Even with a strong running mate [Minneapolis businessman Keith Reitman], my chance of winning was limited because I was a write-in candidate. But I thought Ventura had a good chance to win and I told him so. I suggested that he pace himself and rest along the way so he would be strong and able to represent the ordinary people who really liked him.

He said he didn't expect to win the general election and was only in the race to help the Reform Party achieve five percent of the vote, in order to keep its major party status. He also wanted some publicity for himself.

You should have seen the excitement he generated in St. Cloud, August 1998. After the forum, the crowd ignored the other candidates and surged toward this larger than life hero. Ventura was pleasant and congenial as he signed autograph after autograph and had his picture taken with anyone who wanted one. Kids with their parents were given special attention. Ventura, man of the people, was eating up the adoration.

Ventura's two major adversaries for governor were easy people for the public to reject. The first, Skip Humphrey, was Minnesota's attorney general, an old-school, backroom, deal-making Democrat. The other competitor was DFL turncoat and political opportunist Norm Coleman, then Republican mayor of St. Paul.

NORM "THE BRATTY" AND SKIP "THE BOOBIES" SCRAMBLE TO RECOVER VOTERS LOST TO JESSE "THE BODY"

Humphrey and Coleman represented the political party, favor trading way of doing things and Ventura seemed to represent a "plainer talking, get it done for the people" style. Ventura would poke fun at them by calling them full time politicians. Throughout the course of the campaign, the people chanted support for their newfound hero.   **Jess-ee Jess-ee Jess-ee**

When Ventura's victory was officially announced at the election night party, the excitement and enthusiasm of the crowd was breathtaking. The media was going nuts and Ventura loved it. Jesse "The Body" Ventura had "shocked the world," and now he would lead Minnesota into the new millennium. Hope was high for the future of Minnesota.

I thought he would be good for the people, the environment and the welfare of animals. Good in all ways. Governor Jesse "The Body" Ventura. My hopes were high, along with my fellow Minnesotans. I was excited for his victory.

It was big news all over the county, this amazing Minnesota upset. I hoped Ventura would do fabulous things and I wanted to help him, for all the right reasons, because, "we won."

My opinion of Ventura and my desire to help him changed dramatically when, within seven weeks of his election, he did the following things:

- **Told single mothers they were on their own regarding government help**
- **Shot pheasants that were kept in cages all of their lives, and then released and killed for the pleasure of lazy, blood-lusting hunters**
- **Supported the largest police raid in Minnesota history at Highway 55***

*On December 20, 1998, with the knowledge and approval of governor-elect Ventura, more than 600 state and local police violently descended upon a handful of peaceful protesters who were occupying seven houses that the state wanted to demolish in order to expand Highway 55 in Minneapolis.

During the raid the police arrested 36 people: brutalizing and torturing (see footnote) more than 10 of them. Pepper spray was swabbed into the eyelids of several handcuffed, peaceful individuals. One of the people tortured by the police was Henry Fieldseth, a Minnesota peace activist I have known for 24 years.

The Highway 55 occupation was the longest running urban occupation in American history. The thousands of people who supported and maintained it were ordinary people like you and me.

Supporting organizations included Earth First!, American Indian Movement, Mendota Mdewakaton Tribe, Earth Protectors, Sisters of St. Joseph, Veterans for Peace, Sierra Club, Women's Earth Brigade and many other church groups, small businesses, students, politicians, homemakers, professional people, scientists and property owners. On December 28, 1998, the Minneapolis (MN) *Star Tribune* reported that Ventura spokeswoman Teresa McFarland said Ventura was briefed on the proposed raid by Governor Carlson's administration, and he, Ventura, supported the raid.

TORTURE FOOTNOTE: (Article1, United Nations Convention Against Torture 1984) "For the purpose of this Convention, the term 'torture' means any act by which severe pain or suffering, whether physical or mental, is intentionally inflicted on a person for such purposes of obtaining from him or a third person information or a confession, punishing him for an act he or a third person has committed or is suspected of having committed, or intimidating or coercing him or a third person for any reason based on discrimination of any kind, when such pain or suffering is inflicted by or at the instigation of or with the consent or acquiescence of a public official or other person acting in an official capacity."

Right around this time, a friend of mine, working in the Anoka County Schools, confided to one of her top students that she was upset about the raid. The student told her to, "call Jesse, he'll help."

But Jesse had his own special message he was conveying to students:

> *"Win if you can, lose if you must, but ALWAYS CHEAT."*

On December 30, 1998, I withdrew my support for Ventura and asked his chief of staff to send back my contribution, T-shirt and résumé. He returned these items to me on January 27, 1999.

The largest police raid in Minnesota history.
Highway 55, December 1998

Chapter Two

William "Bill" Dahn
Candidate for Governor of Minnesota

Bill Dahn
From video shot at his house, July 19.

**On July 14, 1998,
Dahn, a political unknown, registered
to run for governor of Minnesota
in the Reform Party.**

July 14   William "Bill" Dahn registers to run for governor in the Reform Party

July 17   Minneapolis *Star Tribune* story headline: ST. PAUL MAN WHO'S TUSSLED WITH CITY TO OPPOSE VENTURA

July 18   *St. Paul Pioneer Press* story headline: VENTURA GETS CHALLENGER IN REFORM PRIMARY

In Minnesota, there is a two-week period in which a person can register to run for governor. In 1998, the registration period was from July 7 to July 21.

On July 14, William "Bill" Dahn registered to run for governor, representing the Reform Party by paying the Minnesota Secretary of State a $600 non-refundable, non-transferable registration fee. Dahn used his mortgage money to pay the $600 fee. (While Ventura did not register to run for governor until one week later, on July 21, he had already announced his intention.)

On July 17, 1998: the *Star Tribune* reported Dahn's registration. In the article Dahn said he admired Ventura and that running against him in the primary would help Ventura. He also said, "I'm going to go through all the information I got and it's going to help him [Ventura], but I'm not gonna let it out right now."

On July 18, 1998: the *St. Paul Pioneer Press* reported Dahn as saying the same thing as the *Star Tribune*.

Both of these articles clearly pointed out that Dahn was exactly where he wanted to be: in the Reform Party running for governor of Minnesota in the September 1998 primary election.

Dahn was a 48 year-old disabled Native American who stuttered severely, lived in a modest white stucco house in St. Paul and got by financially on monthly worker disability payments.

Dahn wanted to run for governor of Minnesota in order to have a platform from which to expose a corrupt government-sponsored weatherization program. The program had contaminated his house with formaldehyde-soaked insulation. He also wanted the public to know how the DFL and Republican gubernatorial candidates, Skip Humphrey and Norm Coleman, were involved in the weather-ization matter, and how they failed to help him.

Dahn's house at 256 Morton Street, St. Paul, Minnesota

When Dahn went to register with the Secretary of State on July 14, he did not know he was required to have a lieutenant governor with him. He left and asked his cousin, James Kane, to fill that post. They returned to the Secretary of State's office with the intention of registering as Libertarians or Independents. They were told that to register as Libertarians or Independents they would need to acquire 2000 signatures by July 21. Rather then rush out and obtain 2000 signatures in seven short days, they chose the option of registering with one of the major parties—the Reform Party.

Dahn's registration guaranteed that he would be on the Reform Party ballot in the September 1998 primary election.

Ventura and Barkley would later say that Dahn was misled or misinformed by the Secretary of State's staff and that he really wanted to register in the Republican Party. It's absurd to think that Dahn is a Republican. He survives on monthly worker disability income, gets his food at a food shelf, advocates for the poor, helps senior citizens and fights for the environment.

Joe Mansky, elections director with the Secretary of State at the time, and Renee Coffey, the clerk who took Dahn's registration and notarized it, both denied that Dahn was misled or misinformed. Mansky and Coffey both stated that they only provided Dahn with the rules for registration and that Dahn had made his own decision.

Ventura and Barkley invented the lie that the Secretary of State misinformed Dahn. They would use that lie numerous times as part of their bribery cover-up.

Chapter Three

Dean Barkley

In 1998, Dean Barkley was Jesse Ventura's campaign committee chairman.

He fixed the 1998 Minnesota primary election and he fixed the outcome of the ensuing investigation.

Dean Barkley is director of the Minnesota Planning Agency. In January 1999, Governor Ventura appointed him to his $97,300 a year position.

An attorney since 1977, Barkley was a key building block of the Minnesota Reform Party. He ran for election to the U.S. House of Representatives in 1992 and the U.S. Senate in 1994 and 1996. Barkley received enough votes in the U.S. Senate race to qualify the Minnesota Reform Party for major status. Major status is very important because it allows a party to obtain state money, and it provides easy and open ballot access for its candidates.

Barkley was a past director of the Common Cause political watchdog group and was considered to be an expert political strategist with a vast knowledge of election laws.

In 1997, Dean Barkley hand-picked Jesse Ventura to be the Reform Party poster boy for the office of governor of Minnesota. They announced Ventura's candidacy in January 1998.

Barkley correctly believed that Ventura could garner at least five percent of the votes cast in the November 1998 general election. Five percent was the "magic" number needed for the Reform Party to retain its major party status.

Barkley was **the person** who put together the team of people who helped Ventura "shock the world" with his victory. Barkley was Ventura's campaign committee chairman and made the important decisions. Doug Friedline was Ventura's campaign manager, Mavis Huddle was campaign secretary, Phil Villaume was the campaign legal counsel and Phil Madsen would do public relations and assorted dirty work.

Barkley was key, and incredibly effective, in bribing Dahn. He mislead the media and fixed the ensuing investigation into his violation of Minnesota Statute 211B.10, Subdivision 1. This law states:

> **"A person may not reward or promise to reward another in an manner to induce the person to be or refrain from or cease being a candidate. A person may not solicit or receive a payment, promise, or reward from another for this purpose."**

As an expert on campaign laws, Barkley was surely aware of the existence of this law when on July 21, 1998, he stood beside Bill Dahn and James Kane as they withdrew their Reform Party candidacy and he paid his own $600 to register them as Republicans.

July 22, 1998, the *Star Tribune* quoted Barkley saying, "they didn't have the money so I wrote a check."

The article goes on to state that Barkley did so, "because of concerns that a Reform Party primary opponent could 'knock Jesse off the air' by invoking federal equal-time broadcast rules."

Also on July 22, Barkley told the *St. Paul Pioneer Press* that, "potentially, if Jesse had an opponent in the primary, the FCC could force him off the air…and Jesse wanted to work as long as he can."

These are clear admissions that Barkley bribed Dahn so Ventura could keep his job as the host of a radio talk show that catered to a sports audience.

Barkley avoided mentioning the additional advantage that the bribe gave Ventura: it eliminated Ventura's competition in the September Reform Party primary.

Two complaints were filed against Barkley for bribing Dahn to withdraw from the Reform Party. An investigation ensued.

On August 6, 1998, Barkley was the first person to be interviewed by investigators.

According to the investigators, Barkley brought attorney Phil Villaume to the interview and they both took detailed notes of the questions asked and answers given. Villaume was one of Ventura's attorneys and is the brother of Barkley's wife.

Barkley wanted to be sure Dahn or his running mate Kane would not contradict the information he provided to investigators. He told them the investigators lacked subpoena authority, and couldn't order them to be interviewed. He said that when the investigators called, they should refuse to be interviewed.

On August 14, 1998, Dahn and Kane telephoned the investigators and declined to be interviewed.

Barkley also told Dahn that if the media questioned him, he should stick with the story about being misled by the Secretary of State's staff on July 14.

On August 25, 1998, investigators interviewed Ventura campaign manager Doug Friedline. Upon completion of his interview, long-time Ramsey County investigator Dennis Hoff asked Friedline if he had collaborated with others to discuss what they would say when questioned because, **"I get the feeling it almost seems like the story is uniform past the point of what it would be if it were true."**

Friedline responded, "we never met as a group and I'm a small part of the picture."

We know that Barkley and Villaume had notes from Barkley's interview with the investigators. Is it believable that Barkley did not share those notes with Friedline?

In the midst of the bribe, the switch and the investigation, something unexpected happened. Ventura became governor. All media hell broke loose, and Barkley went from being a car wash manager with a law degree, to a $97,300 job as Minnesota's planning director.

Chapter Four

The Bribe

James Kane - Jesse Ventura - Bill Dahn
rejoicing after the completed bribe.
From video shot at Dahn's house, July 19.

On July 15, 1998, Jesse Ventura and Dean Barkley learned that Bill Dahn had registered to run for governor in the Reform Party. They did not want Dahn in the Reform Party because it could cause Ventura to lose his job as a radio talk show host, and it would give Ventura competition in the September Reform Party primary election.

They went to Dahn's house and bribed him to withdraw from the Reform Party.

July 15   Doug Friedline (campaign manager)
          learns about Dahn and alerts others

July 16, 17 Friedline speaks with Dahn and Kane
          and reports back to his colleagues

July 17   Friedline arranges a meeting for Ventura
          and Barkley to meet Dahn

July 18   Friedline tells Dahn what Ventura expects
          of him

July 19   Ventura, Barkley, Dahn and Kane meet at
          Dahn's house

July 20   Phil Madsen, a Ventura operative, is
          assigned to be with Dahn for the day

July 21   Ventura registers for governor, and
          shortly thereafter the bribe is executed

Part 1

On July 15, 1998, Doug Friedline, Ventura's campaign manager, was monitoring the Secretary of State's website when he learned that, on July 14, William "Bill" Dahn had officially registered to run for governor of Minnesota on the Reform Party ticket.

Ventura had not yet officially registered his candidacy and would not do so until 2:00 p.m. on July 21, the final day to register.

Friedline immediately notified his colleagues: Ventura, Dean Barkley (campaign chairman) and Mavis Huddle (campaign secretary), that a political unknown had registered in the Reform Party and would run against Ventura in the September primary.

Huddle and Friedline recalled speaking with Dahn. He had called the campaign office numerous times seeking Ventura's help with a problem he was having with his contaminated house. Ventura never returned Dahn's calls. Huddle said she didn't have much information about Dahn but she recalled he was troubled and excitable.

The group agreed that they had to remove Dahn from the Reform Party and they left the details to Friedline and Huddle. Friedline would contact Dahn to gather more information about him, and what it would require to remove him from the Reform Party.

In the ensuing days, Friedline had numerous conversations with Dahn and his running mate, James Kane. By gaining their confidence, Friedline learned all about Dahn's situation. He was certain that Dahn could be convinced to withdraw from the Reform Party if Ventura would help him with the contamination problem he was having with his house.

Based on Friedline's information to the group, a plan was devised that would move Dahn into the Republican Party. They thought this would allow Ventura to stay on the air with his broadcasting job, and eliminate competition from the September Reform Party primary. Friedline got the go ahead and he arranged the meeting with Dahn.

Barkley and Ventura now knew all about Bill Dahn's situation. They knew that Dahn's main concern was that his house was contaminated with formaldehyde due to a faulty government-sponsored weatherization program. They knew that Dahn was disabled, unemployed and living on a small monthly worker disability payment.

They would promise to help Dahn get his house fixed. And since Dahn's $600 Reform Party registration fee was not refundable or transferable, Barkley would pay the new $600 fee so Dahn could register as a Republican and still stay in the race.

Friedline had worked things out on the phone and convinced Dahn that by registering as a Republican he could still fight his enemy, Republican candidate Norm Coleman, who as the mayor of St. Paul had refused to help Dahn with his housing problem. In addition, Dahn would have a forum from which to continue expressing his views on other issues.

The plan was for Ventura to register his candidacy on Tuesday, July 21, at 2:00 p.m. Dahn would withdraw immediately after that, at 3:00 p.m. This way, on the off chance anyone else wanted to challenge Ventura, it would be too late for him or her to learn about the switcheroo and jump in. This guaranteed that Ventura would run unopposed all the way through the September primary election.

Ventura and Barkley would cloud their bribery activity by having Dahn say that the Secretary of State's staff misled him when he initially registered in the Reform party, and he really wanted to register in the Republican Party.

Friedline arranged a meeting for Ventura, Barkley, Dahn and Kane, to meet at Dahn's home on Sunday afternoon, July 19.

Part 2

Just prior to the Sunday, July 19 meeting, Barkley called Dahn to make certain only he and his running mate, James Kane, would be present to meet with him and Ventura.

Ventura would later say that he wanted Barkley along because he thought the meeting would be reported to the media and he wanted a witness to make sure that nobody would think something "fishy" was occurring.

Part 3

It was Sunday afternoon when Ventura's Porsche pulled up and parked on the wrong side of the street, across from Dahn's home, a small white stucco house with a huge crack in the glass front door.

Dahn and Kane watched nervously through the window as an angry looking Ventura struggled out of his sports car and lumbered across the street with Barkley at his side.

Dahn had never met Ventura. He admired him, but he was also afraid of him because he knew Ventura's reputation as a hard ass. Further, Friedline had told Dahn that Ventura was angry with him for registering in the Reform Party.

According to Dahn's sworn affidavit, Ventura and Barkley entered his front door and Ventura immediately growled, "what did I do to piss you guys off?"

Ventura did most of the talking. He told Dahn that his candidacy in the Reform Party would hurt his campaign. He also told Dahn that having a second candidate running on the Reform Party ticket might cause him to lose his job as host of a call-in show on KFAN sports radio due to Federal Communications Commission (FCC) equal airtime rules for candidates. He told Dahn that he needed the radio job to support his family. Friedline would later tell investigators that he had discussed Ventura's radio show with Dahn, and Dahn had agreed to sign a waiver of his right to equal airtime.

Dahn told Ventura that he didn't mean to hurt his chances but he wanted to be in the race to have a forum to express his issues and expose the problems with his house. He told Ventura about the problems with his house and how gubernatorial candidates Humphrey (DFL) and Coleman (GOP) had refused to help him.

Friedline and Huddle had already briefed Ventura about Dahn but Ventura listened for awhile anyway. After a few minutes, Ventura laid it on the line.

He told Dahn that he wanted him out of the Reform Party and that he must withdraw. Barkley would pay the $600 fee to register him as a Republican, and as a Republican he could still have his issues heard.

In a video recording made at the close of the meeting at Dahn's house, Ventura said, "we'll plan then, on Tuesday at 3 o'clock, you guys are gonna go over with Dean and switch to become Republicans. We're gonna switch you—we're gonna switch you to being Republican. We'll switch you—you're gonna be

Republicans now. All you gotta do is walk in there and say 'I am a Republican.'"

Jesse Ventura and Bill Dahn
shaking on the bribe.
From video shot at Dahn's house, July 19.

Dahn agreed to withdraw his candidacy and Barkley would be standing by to pay the $600 fee to register him as a Republican.

In addition to paying Dahn's new $600 Republican registration fee, Ventura and Barkley promised to get his house fixed, give him free campaign T-shirts, free washes at Barkley's car wash and they would take him on the road with their campaign. And, if Ventura was elected in November, Dahn could attend the victory party. Also, they would find jobs for him and his friends in the administration.

Ventura and Barkley told Dahn and Kane that if they were asked any questions about the switcheroo, they were to say that they wanted to file as Republicans originally, but were misinformed by the person at the Secretary of State's office, and they were just correcting the matter.

Renee Coffey was the person at the Secretary of State's office who took Dahn's original registration and notarized it. She vividly recalls what occurred and she refutes the claim that Dahn was misinformed.

The day after the meeting at Dahn's house, Phil Madsen, a Ventura operative, was assigned to look after Dahn to make sure he stayed in line. Madsen took Dahn out to eat and kept his eye on him for the day.

Things went according to plan.

Two days after Ventura and Barkley visited Dahn at his house, Ventura registered for governor, Dahn withdrew his Reform Party candidacy and Barkley paid $600 for Dahn to register as a Republican.

Bill Dahn and James Kane received their campaign T-shirts. Barkley also followed through on his promise for free car washes. But Barkley failed to get Dahn's house repaired or find jobs for Dahn and his friends in the administration. In fact, Dahn lost his house. He now lives in a small room of a house owned by a local church.

Part 4

In a Subsequent Investigation, Ventura and Barkley Would Tell the Following Lies:

Barkley said he first learned about Dahn by reading it in the newspaper on July 15. Notice of Dahn's candidacy did not appear in the newspaper until July 17, 1998.

Ventura said he knew nothing about Dahn prior to the meeting at Dahn's house, and that he went to see Dahn to find out why he was running against him. Ventura already knew about Dahn because Friedline and Huddle briefed him. Huddle told him about Dahn's earlier calls to the campaign office and Friedline told him what he learned from his calls to Dahn prior to the meeting at Dahn's house.

Barkley said that he paid Dahn's new $600 registration fee because he felt the system screwed Dahn and he felt sorry for him.

Later, Barkley would tell a different story:

On July 22, 1998, the *Star Tribune* quoted Barkley saying, "'they didn't have the money so I wrote a check.' Why? Because of concerns that a Reform Party primary opponent could 'knock Jesse off the air' by invoking federal equal airtime broadcast rules. With no challenger, Ventura's radio job should be safe until after the primary."

Ventura and Barkley both told investigators that they simply helped Dahn do what he really wanted to do in the first place—to register in the Republican Party.

When the investigators pressed Ventura for details about why he wanted to help Dahn, Ventura blurted out of nowhere that he got sick with severe headaches in Dahn's house on July 19. He magnified this lie by saying that after about 20 minutes, Barkley also got sick and they had to finish their meeting outside. The video taken in Dahn's house shows that the meeting concluded in Dahn's living room.

The day after the bribe, talk show host Joe Soucheray interviewed Ventura:

Soucheray: "You bought the guy."

Ventura: "And the point is—so what if we did that? What's the big deal about it?"

Jesse Ventura
From video shot at Dahn's house, July 19.

When one listens to the Ramsey County investigative taped interviews of Friedline, Barkley and Ventura, reads Barkley's statements in the newspapers, reads the transcript of Ventura's interview with Joe Soucheray, and watches the video taken in Dahn's house—one is left with no doubt that Ventura and Barkley went to Bill Dahn's' house on Sunday, July 19, 1998, and intimidated, coerced and bribed him, to leave the Reform Party.

By bribing Dahn, Ventura and Barkley knowingly violated Minnesota Statute 211B.10 which carries a large fine and possible jail time.

This was not an auspicious start to Ventura's future administration.

Chapter Five

Radio Show

In July 1998, Ventura was host of a daily radio show.

Ventura's contract with KFAN radio allowed it to terminate his job when he officially registered for governor.

On July 21, 1998, Ventura registered for governor at 2:00 p.m. and at 6:00 p.m., *the same day*, his radio job was terminated.

In the mid- to late-1990s, Ventura's popularity and recognition had waned significantly from his earlier heydays. His dual careers in wrestling and acting were virtually non-existent. The only regular work he had in 1997 was hosting a 5:00 a.m. talk show on KSTP radio based in Maplewood, Minnesota.

The KSTP job required Ventura to leave his home by 4:00 a.m., in order to get to the radio station and be on the air by 5:00 a.m. The early show time was wearing on Ventura, and caused him to become exceedingly irritable, even belligerent. His behavior eventually caused KSTP to fire him.

Shortly after KSTP fired Ventura, KFAN radio hired him to cater to their sports listeners, who liked Ventura's antagonistic style. His ratings were good.

According to Mick Anselmo, KFAN vice president, prior to coming to work for KFAN, Ventura told them that he was contemplating running for governor in 1998. KFAN tailored its contract with Ventura to read that if there was a "problem" after he officially registered his candidacy for governor, KFAN could terminate his job. If there was no problem, Ventura could stay on the air.

The problem it was referring to was a Federal Communications Commission (FCC) equal airtime rule for political candidates. The FCC rule forbids political candidates from having free airtime that would give them an unfair advantage over other candidates.

Ventura would later tell investigators that he called the FCC to determine what their rules were on equal airtime for candidates. He said that the FCC told him that if no one filed a complaint, it would not interfere. Ventura said the FCC is reactive, not proactive.

Enter political candidate Bill Dahn. If Dahn requested equal airtime on KFAN, they would have a problem.

Friedline would later tell investigators that he spoke with Dahn about the FCC equal airtime problem and Dahn told him he would sign a waiver stating he would not ask for equal airtime.

On the day Ventura registered, July 21, Doug Westerman, manager of KFAN radio, received a fax from Dick Franson, DFL candidate for secretary of state, which said, "if your station doesn't take Jesse Ventura 'off the air' effective July 22, 1998, I will urge the Federal Communication Commission to grant all candidates for state-wide office 'equal time' on your station, KFAN."

The Federal Communications Act states that: "If any licensee shall permit any person who is a legally qualified candidate for public office to use a broadcasting station, he shall afford equal opportunities to all other such candidates for that office."

Franson made it known publicly that he would complain to the FCC if any candidate had his or her own radio show. He sent a copy of his KFAN fax to radio talk show host, Joe Soucheray.

Soucheray interviewed Ventura on July 22, saying, "I'll tell you why you're not on the air. I'm holding a letter from Dick Franson, to KFAN, saying they better take you off the air or Franson was going to sue them." Ventura responded: "I tell you what, if you want someone with no credibility, try him."

Dick Franson

Franson is a highly decorated retired U.S. Army master sergeant who served with distinction in Korea and Vietnam. Ventura disliked Franson because he had exposed the facts that Ventura was not a SEAL while on active duty in the Navy, and that he never saw combat in Vietnam.

At 6:00 p.m., on July 21, the day Ventura "officially registered" for governor, Mick Anselmo announced that Ventura's employment with KFAN had been terminated.

On July 23, 1998, the *Star Tribune* reported that Anselmo said, "I don't think I would want to allow any political candidate a platform that some would interpret as an unfair advantage."

On July 23, 1998, the *St. Paul Pioneer Press* reported that Anselmo told the Associated Press that, "he removed Ventura from his radio program out of 'fairness to the election process.'" In the same article, **"Ventura said he thought the station was not legally bound to offer other candidates equal time on the radio because he has no Reform Party opponent in the September 15 primary election."**

Anselmo said that he agreed with the terms of federal communications law, but said giving a political candidate a regular platform was not the right thing to do. Anselmo also said that, "objectively, the proper course of action is not to have him on the air until after November."

Ventura said, "I thought last night [July 21] we were home free, and they called me at 6:00 and said 'we're exercising the option to suspend you.'"

Franson's unexpected move spoiled Barkley and Ventura's maneuver to finesse extra radio time for Ventura. Worse, on July 28, 1998, the *Star Tribune* reported that Barkley had been, "lambasted...and reported to prosecutors by GOP leaders for possible campaign law violations." The article criticized Barkley for throwing "money down the drain." It stated that, "Dean Barkley seems not to have reaped much bang for the $600 bucks he plunked down last week."

Nonetheless, Barkley was described as remaining "upbeat," stating, "my main motivation was to allow these people [Dahn and Kane] to do what they wanted to do. Maybe I'm a fool because I believe their story. But I am an underdog kind-of guy."

Chapter Six

Executing the Bribe

On July 21, 1998,
the stage was set at the Secretary of
State's office for the bribe.

Barkley meets with elections director Mansky.

Ventura and Mae Schunk register their candidacy.

Dahn "withdraws" from the Reform Party.

Barkley pays $600 to register Dahn as a Republican.

KFAN radio announces that Ventura is off the air.

July 21   10:30 a.m. Barkley meets with Joe
Mansky, State elections director

2:00 p.m. Ventura and Schunk register

2:30 p.m. Barkley alerts the media to the
switcheroo

3:00 p.m. Dahn withdraws from the
Reform Party with Barkley standing by
to pay Dahn's $600 fee to register as a
Republican

6:00 p.m. KFAN radio announces that
Ventura's job is off the air

Tuesday, July 21, 1998, was two days after the meeting
at Dahn's house, and the last day to register for
governor of Minnesota.

That morning, Barkley began to set up the fix by
meeting with Joe Mansky, Secretary of State elections
director. Barkley met with Mansky to make certain that
things would go smoothly when Dahn and Kane
arrived to do the switcheroo.

Barkley told Mansky that Dahn would be arriving
later in the day to withdraw from the Reform Party
and register as a Republican. Barkley said that
because Mansky's staff misled Dahn when he
originally registered, Dahn should be allowed to
transfer his previous $600 fee and apply it to register
as a Republican. Mansky denied that Dahn was
misled and told Barkley that Dahn would have to
pay another $600 fee.

Barkley is an expert at campaign law. He already knew that Dahn's previous $600 filing fee was not refundable or transferable and it was his intention to pay the new $600 fee since the meeting at Dahn's house. Barkley met with Mansky to establish the "Dahn was misled" smokescreen that he would use later in the day when the media arrived.

From the Sunday meeting at Dahn's house, Barkley knew Dahn had used mortgage money to pay the $600 Reform Party registration fee and was now broke.

Ventura told investigators that he DID NOT ask Dahn where he got the $600 to register because he "didn't think it was any of his business." But Barkley told investigators that Ventura DID ask Dahn where he got the money to register.

Even if Dahn were not broke, it would be ridiculous to think that he would spend another $600 to file as a Republican when he was already in the Reform Party and in the race. Dahn told the media several times that he registered in the Reform Party to help Ventura.

"WOW! THESE JESSE VENTURA ACTION FIGURES ARE SELLING LIKE HOTCAKES!"

Star Tribune and *St. Paul Pioneer Press* articles of July 17, 1998 and July 18, 1998, reported Dahn's registration and made no mention that Dahn was misinformed or misled by the Secretary of State. The articles clearly confirm that Dahn was satisfied with his party affiliation and that he was going to help Ventura by being in the Reform Party.

Barkley had to figure out a way to pay Dahn's new filing fee so it would not look like a bribe. His questions to Mansky were a smokescreen to set the stage for the phony story he would later tell the media. That story was that Dahn really wanted to register as a Republican but he was confused at the Secretary of State's office when he registered.

At 2:00 p.m., Ventura and Mae Schunk registered for governor and lieutenant governor in the Reform Party and Schunk left the capitol grounds immediately. There is no evidence to indicate that Schunk knew anything about the bribes to Dahn.

Immediately after Ventura registered, he held a short meeting with Barkley and Friedline to confirm that Dahn was under control. Barkley assured him that Dahn would be arriving at 3:00 p.m. to execute the bribery arrangement. Ventura and Friedline then left the capitol grounds.

The 3:00 p.m. time on Tuesday was strategically selected for Dahn to complete the switch because it was the final hour of the last day to register. It would be too late for anyone to learn about Dahn's withdrawal and jump in the race to challenge Ventura in the Reform Party September primary.

While awaiting Dahn's arrival at the Secretary of State's office, Barkley went across the street to the media offices in the State capitol building and advised news reporters of his intention to pay $600 for Dahn to register as a Republican.

The media followed Barkley back to the Secretary of State's office where they found Dahn completing his paperwork to "withdraw" his candidacy from the Reform Party. Upon completion of the "withdrawal" papers, Dahn filed as a Republican and Barkley paid the $600 filing fee.

Barkley thought that by being out in the open with the media they wouldn't think he was doing anything wrong. After all, he's a lawyer, businessman, former political candidate and chairman of Ventura's campaign. Would he call the media to witness him bribing Dahn right out in the open? He not only would, he did. Then he lied, lied and lied.

Barkley told the media that he paid the $600 for Dahn to register as a Republican because that's what Dahn really wanted to do all along. Barkley also said that since Dahn was "screwed" by the system, and misled by the Secretary of State's staff, he was going to pay $600 from his personal account in order to correct the injustice done to Dahn. Barkley and Ventura would repeat that blatant lie repeatedly during an ensuing investigation.

To help with the cover-up, Ventura and Barkley told Dahn that if the media questioned him about his "withdrawal," he should say that he was misled at the Secretary of State's office when he registered on July 14th. Dahn was to say he wanted to register as a Republican but the clerk would not let him.

The clerk at the time was Ms. Renee Coffey, who says she was the person who received Dahn's Affidavit of Candidacy and notarized it. Ms. Coffey has a very clear recollection of Dahn and Kane coming into her office and being provided with the facts of registration, as her job requires her to do. She firmly asserts that she did not bias them in any way and she had no vested interest in influencing them. She clearly recalls that once Dahn and Kane had the information, they made their decision to register in the Reform Party.

Joe Mansky, elections director for the Secretary of State, confirmed this. Mansky denied that Dahn was misled. He told the *Star Tribune* (July 22, 1998), "we don't advise candidates, we just tell them what the law is." Mansky said Dahn could have registered as a Republican or Democrat just as well as the Reform Party and he chose the Reform Party.

In the same July 22 *Star Tribune* article, Dahn stated that he filed as a Reform party candidate to help Ventura's campaign. Dahn would later explain that he planned to give Ventura some negative information about Republican gubernatorial candidate Norm Coleman.

A *St. Paul Pioneer Press* article (July 18, 1998), gave no indication that Dahn was in the wrong party or that he wanted to be a Republican. Dahn told the newspaper that he was running to expose corruption over a government financed weatherization program. Dahn had been saying for several years that when candidate Norm Coleman was mayor of St. Paul he knew about the corrupt weatherization program and helped cover it up.

With Dahn's withdrawal complete, he, his running mate Kane, Ventura and Barkley, were all now guilty of violating Minnesota Statute 211B.10, which prohibits bribing a candidate to withdraw...or a candidate taking a bribe to withdraw.

Ventura and Barkley now had Dahn and Kane in their corrupt web. They would have to play ball or get punished for taking a bribe. They might even have to pay a large fine and possibly go to jail.

Chapter Seven

Days Following the Bribe

Media reaction to the bribe is swift.

Newspapers and radio talk shows jump on the issue.

Two bribery complaints are filed.

July 22   *Star Tribune* story headline:
COLEMAN FACES CHALLENGERS;
VENTURA DOESN'T

July 22   *St. Paul Pioneer Press* story headline:
CANDIDATE FILING ENDS WITH A
MISS AND A SWITCH

July 22   Joe Soucheray of KSTP-AM radio
interviews Ventura

July 23   Dick Franson files a bribery complaint
with Ramsey County attorney, Susan
Gaertner

July 24   Minnesota Republican Party also files a
bribery complaint

Part 1

July 22, 1998: the *Star Tribune* reported that Barkley paid $600 for Dahn and Kane to register as Republicans. The article quoted Barkley saying, "they didn't have the money so I wrote a check." Why? Because of concerns that a Reform primary opponent could "knock Jesse off the air" by invoking federal equal-time broadcast rules. With no challenger, Ventura's radio job should be safe until after the primary.

July 22, 1998: the *St. Paul Pioneer Press* reported that Barkley paid $600 for Dahn to register as a Republican after withdrawing from the Reform Party, because, "potentially, if Jesse had an opponent in the primary, the FCC could force him off the air [due to equal time rules] and Jesse wanted to work as long as he can."

These statements prove that Barkley bribed Dahn so Ventura could stay on the air.

July 22, 1998: Joe Soucheray, host of a KSTP-AM radio show, interviewed Ventura about bribing Dahn. In the interview Ventura admits that he "bought off" Bill Dahn so he wouldn't have competition in the September primary.

A partial transcript of the Soucheray interview:

Joe Soucheray: If you didn't have a radio show and you were just a guy running do you think that Dean Barkley would have gone and paid the $600 bucks so this guy would have gotten himself into the right party?

Jesse Ventura: So what.

Soucheray: Look, you've already agreed with me on the generic point.

Ventura: Absolutely, Joe.

Soucheray: **You bought the guy.**

Ventura: The bigger point is this; the point is he would have never run against me in the first place if there hadn't been the problem. You know, at the Secretary of State's office. He wouldn't have ran against me, he wanted to run against Coleman, that's who he's got the beef with, that's who he's got the showdown with. And the point is, **so what if we did that? What's the big deal about it?**

Soucheray: **Which had the additional convenience of getting him off the Reform Party's ticket under the assumption that it would have cleared the way for you to remain on the radio.**

Ventura: **Well, okay Joe maybe so.**

Two complaints were filed as a result of Barkley
and Ventura bribing Dahn to withdraw from the
Reform Party.

Dick Franson filed one of those complaints. Franson is
a highly decorated retired U.S. Army master sergeant,
who served with distinction in the Korean and
Vietnam Wars. Franson has a BA degree in public
administration, is a former elected Minneapolis
alderman (councilman) and a former U.S. federal
appraiser. At the time Franson filed his complaint, he
was a DFL candidate for the office of Minnesota
secretary of state.

July 23, 1998: Dick Franson filed his complaint with
Ramsey County attorney Susan Gaertner, alleging that
Dean Barkley violated Minnesota Statute 211.B10 by
inducing Bill Dahn to withdraw his candidacy from
the Reform Party. Franson requested that a "full investigation should be conducted according to law."

The Minnesota Republican Party also filed a complaint
on July 24, 1998. Their complaint was similar to
Franson's and also requested an investigation.
An investigation ensued.

Part 2

And so it went. Article after article and interview
after interview bemoaned the bribe. Yet Ventura and
Barkley stuck with their stories that someone at the
Secretary of State's office confused Dahn and that
they were just trying to help him correct the
unfairness. Barkley said he felt empathy for Dahn.

According to State elections director Joe Mansky, there was no unfairness and no confusion at the Secretary of State's office. Mansky and his staff person Renee Coffey both stated numerous times that Dahn was treated fairly, was well informed and that he made his own decision to register in the Reform Party. Coffey said that she took Dahn's Reform Party registration and notarized it.

Dahn knew exactly what he was doing when he used his mortgage money for the $600 registration fee. He filed for office in order to get in the race and have a platform from which to express his issues, and to expose a corrupt government weatherization program.

Ventura and Barkley claimed that after Dahn withdrew from the Reform Party, he remained a candidate by registering as a Republican. They said they simply helped him re-file.

The fact that Dahn registered in another party after withdrawing is irrelevant. The crime took place at the exact time Dahn "withdrew" because of the bribe.

No re-filing or re-registration can erase the fact that Ventura and Barkley violated Minnesota law by interfering with Dahn's right to run for public office in the party of his choice.

Part 3

THE COMPLAINTS

The complaints were filed with Ramsey County [Minnesota] attorney Susan Gaertner because Ramsey County is where the alleged crime occurred.

The very moment Gaertner received the complaints she had a conflict of interest and should have immediately sent the matter to another county for disposition.

Gaertner's conflict was that her lover, and $90,000 per year employee, John Wodele, was a friend of Dean Barkley, the subject of the complaints.

When Wodele ran for mayor of Minneapolis in 1993, Barkley supported his campaign and got him the Reform Party endorsement.

WHO IS SUSAN GAERTNER?

WHY DID SHE VIOLATE HER ELECTED OFFICE?

Chapter Eight

The Complaints

Susan Gaertner

Ramsey County Attorney Susan Gaertner used her elected office to fix the bribery investigation.

Kathleen Greening murder controversy.

Susan Gaertner's romantic relationship with John Wodele.

Susan Gaertner

Gaertner graduated from the University of Minnesota Duluth in 1976. She completed law school at the University of Minnesota and passed the bar in 1980. She trained for two years as a law clerk for a federal judge, and worked less than two years for a private law firm.

In 1984, the 29 year-old, wide-eyed former Girl Scout and school newspaper editor landed a job at the office of the Ramsey County attorney. She would be an assistant county attorney prosecutor working for Tom Foley.

Gaertner arrived at Foley's office in the midst of the Kathleen Greening murder controversy. Allegations were being made that her boss, Tom Foley, had covered up or misdirected the murder investigation of Kathleen Greening.

In 1982, Kathleen Greening, 33, was found dead in the bathtub of her Lauderdale, Minnesota home. The cause of her death was classified as "undetermined."

Carol Kellogg, a close friend of Greening's, insisted that her friend was murdered. It would take Kellogg four long years of dedicated effort to have her friend's death classified as a murder.

What changed from 1982 when Greening's death was classified as "undetermined" to 1986 when it was reclassified as "murder?"

The Greening murder is described on the next few pages to give the reader a perspective of the work environment that Gaertner entered into in 1984.

KATHLEEN GREENING MURDER

Kathleen Greening

A little after 9:00 a.m. on July 21, 1982, Kathleen Greening was late picking up her friend, Carol Kellogg, for a trip to Mackinac Island. By 9:30, Kellogg started to worry. She called Greening's home but there was no answer. More time passed and Kellogg was certain that her friend must have had an accident. She called Greening's mother and hospitals along the route from Greening's home in Lauderdale, Minnesota to her home in Hudson, Wisconsin. No one had seen or heard from her.

By midday Kellogg decided to drive to Greening's home to learn what she could. When she arrived at the house she saw that Greening's car was there, but when she knocked no one answered the door. A neighbor who looked after Greening's dog had a key to her house and let Kellogg in.

What Kellogg found would eventually result in the most controversial and mind boggling murder case in Minnesota history.

Kellogg entered the house with the neighbor and when her friend didn't answer her calls, she began to search the house. She found Greening's naked body in the bathtub, on her back, dead, with her head facing toward the faucet end of the tub. The immediate thought in the mind of Kellogg, an intelligent school-teacher, was murder. Her friend had been murdered.

However, the cause of death was officially classified as "undetermined" by the Ramsey County medical examiner's office. Kellogg tried to get the medical examiner to reclassify the "undetermined" finding to murder so it could be investigated properly. She was not successful.

OFFICE OF THE MEDICAL EXAMINER
County of Ramsey.
State of. Minnesota

MEMORANDUM

TO: Erhard Haus, M.D., Ph.D.
         Medical Examiner

FROM: Michael B. McGee, M.D.
         Assistant Medical Examiner

DATE: August 12, 1982

SUBJ: Kathy Greening ME82-712

      Dr. Haus, enclosed find a summary of a case our office is currently investigating. (Initially this was felt to be a possible suicide by oral ingestion of drugs. In view of our findings I feel it may represent a homicide.)
      Please read over and return to the ME office. This is an ongoing investigation, the police ask that no comment be made regarding our findings. The husband is a local attorney and may contact you at your office.

      3) The husband and deceased woman have been seperated for some time and are in the process of undergoing a divorce. The husband has a history of violence toward the wife, was paying $900.00/month support, and was in a hurry to make a settlement. All of these allegations are brought forth by the deceased woman's attorney whose statement I include for your review.
      4) The police department investigator believes the scene has been arranged, is too neat, with no water on the floor, no towel, etc. Furthermore, they indicate the husband may be a primary suspect.

COMMENT
      Photographs are available and are being copied for our office. Viewing the subject lying in the bath tub gives the distinct impression that she was placed there.
      This case may represent a suicide, however, her emotional state prior to death, planned vacation, numbers of pills at scene, etc. do not really support this. Given her position in the tub, I do not believe she could have fallen into the water and assumed her final position. Therefore, based on the information we now have I feel the case is best signed out <u>undetermined</u>.

Michael B. McGee, M.D.
Assistant Medical Examine

ck

**Excerpted from Dave Racer's Minnesota Report
November 1988**

Extensive phone conversations between Carol Kellogg
and an assistant Ramsey County medical examiner in
1986 give a painfully vivid impression that public and
appointed officials viewed the Kathy Greening murder
case as a time-consuming bother that would probably
remain unsolved.

Dialogue between Kellogg and James Essling of the
medical examiner's office leave no mistake how investigators and lawyers assigned to the case felt about it:
they hoped it would go away.

These are some impressions gleaned from the
emotional, and at times maudlin, remarks Essling
made to Kellogg on February 17, 1986, and again
10 days later when he telephoned her.

Minnesota Report has excerpted remarks from the
conversations.

Essling asked Kellogg how she was holding up in her
nerve-fraying fight to get Greening's manner of death
reclassified by medical examiner Michael McGee.

*"I'm fine," she replied, and then asked Essling the same
question.*

*Essling, a longtime coroner's assistant, replied, "it scares me,
I guess," referring to the murder and its political sensitivity.*

*Kellogg: "Why? You deal with it [murder] all the time. Why
should it scare you?"*

Essling: "We don't deal with this all the time. This is very different. You have to be a practical person and I live in a practical world..."

Essling was referring to a news-hungry local media that had acquired an interest in Kellogg's complaints. Essling told her he feared friction was inevitable between the examiner's office and Ramsey County attorney's office because of the glare of publicity.

The offices must get along well because they do business daily, he said, yet they found themselves posturing after Kellogg's first flurry of publicity.

McGee initially had labeled the manner of Greening's death a "possible fresh water drowning." He later made a finding of "undetermined" and even later, fully three and a half years after her death, McGee called it "homicide."

At the time Essling phoned her, however, Kellogg was still two weeks away from successfully forcing the homicide determination.

By then, officials were giving her a Catch-22 explanation that no doubt turned her curiosity into a crusade; there could be no investigation until there is a crime; and since McGee wouldn't call it a crime...

Kellogg replied almost angrily after Essling related how he gave the Greening file "to five lawyers—and it came back four to one [for homicide]." But there was a problem, Essling pointed out: "How are they [Foley's office] ever gonna prosecute this?"

Kellogg blurted almost derisively: "Jim, it's never been investigated."

And to be sure, it hadn't. If you listen to the litany of Kellogg complaints about police and lawyer bungling, you will understand why. A sampling:

- Roseville police failed to seal off the murder house adequately, then gave keys to the place to the chief suspect three hours later.

- Police were sloppy in pinpointing the alibis of key suspects.

- Investigators virtually ignored the fact that the bedroom had been the scene of a fierce struggle.

- Doctors did a poor job of autopsying Greening's remains, said Kellogg, failing to notice a bump over her eyebrow, a cut on the bridge of her nose and a deep blue, thumbprint shaped bruise on her neck.

- The Minnesota Attorney General's office impeded rather then helped the murder investigation and helped Foley short-circuit an attempt to take a closer look at Greening's finances.

Kellogg made a tape recording of a visit to discuss Kathy Greening with Attorney General Hubert H. Humphrey III. Humphrey told the dead woman's mother and Kellogg that investigators and lawyers on the case are "fine professionals." Beyond that Humphrey offered no help, stating his office didn't deal with street crimes.

Later in the conversation with Kellogg, Essling hinted
that he and McGee were about [to] "go to war" with
the county attorney's office over the death certificate
classification. He belittled the financial information
showing that the victim's husband stood to benefit
from the death financially, saying it wasn't useful as
evidence in a crime.

*"So he benefited greatly by it [Kathy's death]…big deal.
Everything points to murder. If you were unbiased and
sitting on a jury, you'd have to…uh, you know, beyond the
reasonable doubt…that's the ultimate, I guess."*

Kellogg: "So you sit on it and nothing happens?"

*Essling: "No, no, no! We're gonna do something about
it…but number one, what more can they [Foley and the
police] do? I ask you?"*

*Kellogg: (Bewildered, now shouting in disbelief): "What
more can they do…what more? They can call it a homicide.
Tell the truth."*

Intimating that politics and outsiders had prevailed in
influencing McGee's decision, Kellogg waited for
Essling's angered reply.

*Essling: "Nobody ever gets to me…you've got that all
wrong…I'm gonna do what I'm gonna do but the doctor
[McGee] will take the big brunt of it because they're gonna
ask us why…"*

*Kellogg: "Jim, you said yourself that the county attorney
didn't want to see it come back [to Foley's office as a
homicide demanding prosecution]…"*

Essling: "…The thing that (expletive) me off the most…this guy [McGee] I work with: I like him I respect him…he feels the same way…"

Kellogg: "And just how does he feel?"

Essling (clearing his throat): "That we have to do something."

Kellogg: "Do something like change the cause of death?"

Essling: "Not the cause of death."

Kellogg: "Okay, the manner of death."

Essling (pausing for a moment): "So…we get it done and take some heat…"

Kellogg asked about two meetings his office had with Foley's office. She asked: "What happened?"

Essling: "They asked us not to…"

Kellogg: "What?"

Essling: "The county attorney asked us not to."

Kellogg: "The county attorney asked you not to?"

Essling (affirming that the request had been made): "Uh huh."

At one point, Essling told Kellogg that examiner McGee shook his head in anger when a state attorney phoned to tell Essling the state would have no involvement unless Foley ordered it.

"He's covering it up, Jim." McGee murmured, as the attorney's voice coursed through the offices at Ramsey County Morgue. Essling had put the call on a speaker-phone for all to hear.

Essling summed up his frustration about the Greening case toward the end of one of the phone calls this way: "We all blew the case, Carol," he said. **[End Racer Report]**

Kellogg would mount a multi-year effort to have the death reclassified and bring the murderer(s) to justice. In 1986, she brought the case to the attention of the I-Team, a part of the Minneapolis-based news station WCCO-TV. After a lengthy investigation by the I-Team they broadcasted their findings.

The I-Team would allege that Ramsey County attorney Tom Foley had requested medical examiner, Dr. Michael McGee, not to reclassify the Greening case as a murder and that he also blocked a proper investigation for political reasons. The I-Team suggested that a suspect in the case had donated money to Foley's campaign and was connected with a prominent Minnesota law firm closely connected to Foley's election campaign.

On the eve of the I-Team's broadcast, after four years, Dr. McGee reclassified the Greening case as a murder.

That same day, Tom Foley and his clever media-spinning spokesman, John Wodele, arranged a news conference at which Foley declared that he had a conflict of interest in the Greening murder case. He said that he was sending the case to Anoka County for an investigation. Anoka County eventually presented the case to a grand jury and no one was charged.

Foley would later file a defamation lawsuit against
WCCO-TV in Hennepin County District Court.
Foley lost. Upon receiving Judge Schiefelbein's
decision, Foley's spokesman and executive assistant,
John Wodele, said that Foley was out of town but,
"undoubtedly would be disappointed with the
ruling and might consider an appeal." Foley did
appeal to the Minnesota Court of Appeals and lost.
He then appealed to the Supreme Court and lost
again. It was over for now.

Kellogg kept the pressure on through the 1980s to
bring her friend's murderer to justice. She sought
the help of Attorney General Skip Humphrey and
his Solicitor General Norm Coleman. Kellogg said
they did more to hinder her effort than help.
(Coleman and Humphrey ran for governor in 1998
and lost to Ventura.)

She hired a private investigator and an attorney. She
nagged state officials until they appointed an investigator. When the investigator was making headway
he was taken off the case. Conversations were
recorded and played for the media. Newspapers,
magazines and television shows (Inside Edition,
WCCO-TV), smelling corruption, cronyism, political
backbiting and a murder cover up, reported
hungrily. On and on Kellogg went, seeking justice
for her murdered friend.

In 1991 she convinced a very willing Republican
Governor Arne Carlson to help. Carlson asked
Republican U.S. attorney Thomas Heffelfinger to
conduct a federal investigation into both the murder
and the alleged cover-up.

Heffelfinger was a buddy of Carlson's and took part in his 1990 election campaign. In 1993 Heffelfinger did legal work for Carlson's 1994 re-election campaign, which Carlson won.

Howls went up from Foley and others...*politics!* they screamed. They were claiming that Carlson was using this opportunity to attack potential opponents, and the federal prosecutor had no business getting involved in the murder.

Heffelfinger would not be deterred. He said his task was to determine whether a provable murder existed and to decide whether criminal misconduct charges should be filed against any public officials. More important, he said, it was "the right thing to do."

Heffelfinger eventually decided not to file charges, closed the case and would not discuss it with anyone, claiming that is was against his policy to tell anyone about a closed investigation that did not yield criminal charges. However, it was reported that Heffelfinger gave a three-hour explanation of his decision to a sobbing Kellogg, the loyal friend of the murdered woman.

By 1994 and 1995 things were simmering down and the Greening murder seemed to be fading away as an unsolved crime. Kellogg was tiring but still pushing against incredible political forces. Even she, while not beaten, had to admit that it was likely that someone would get away with the murder of her friend.

Suddenly, in December 1997, a convicted killer, Paul Stephani, living in a hole at the Oak Park Heights, Minnesota maximum-security prison, confessed to killing Kathleen Greening 15 years earlier.

The police announced the confession at a news conference on December 19, 1997, just before the Christmas and New Years holidays, and the start of the 1998 election season that would see Coleman, Humphrey, Foley and Gaertner seeking office again.

The police said that Stephani confessed to Greening's murder without encouragement. They didn't explain why he didn't recognize her picture. Didn't know the name of the bar where he met her. Didn't know where the bar was. Didn't explain why the police in 1986 didn't find phone numbers in Greening's phone book that they conveniently found now. The police said that Stephani knew things that only the killer would know...but they didn't say what those things were.

Paul Stephani was an incarcerated killer known as the "weepy-voiced killer" because he would call police after his murders and beg that they stop him. He decided to confess after he learned that he had terminal cancer and "wanted to clear the air" before he died. [*St. Paul Pioneer Press*, August 20, 1997.] Or at least get a cell with a window.

The *Pioneer Press* article also reported that two psychiatrists had differing opinions about Stephani's mental condition in 1979. One said Stephani "was a paranoid schizophrenic and he wanted him committed to the St. Peter State Hospital as mentally ill and dangerous to others."

Another psychiatrist said Stephani wasn't a danger to society. And on that opinion James Finley, Ramsey County Probate Court commissioner released Stephani to begin his murder spree.

A psychologist I consulted with analyzed Stephani's confession and found it suspect. She reviewed various pieces of information and spoke with at least one person who viewed a videotape of his confession. It was the psychologist's opinion that the psychiatrist who diagnosed Stephani as paranoid schizophrenic in 1979 was correct. That is why she finds Stephani's confession to be suspect.

The *Pioneer Press* article quoted Stephani, "I could put myself in the (victim's) father's place...How would I feel if I never heard that somebody who killed my daughter had never been in jail or had been caught?...I would be happy to hear he was caught or confessed to it or something. I mean, that is the least I can do even to make them feel better."

My consulting psychologist said that a paranoid schizophrenic such as Stephani would not have the ability to "feel" for the father of his victims. In addition, Stephani's modus operandi (m.o.) does not fit the Greening murder. Stephani was a brutally violent sexual predator, and Greening's asphyxia prior to being put in the bathtub is inconsistent with the evidence, common sense, or Stephani's m.o.

After reviewing many hours of information and evidence in Kathleen Greening's 1982 murder, the psychologist told me that, "whether Stephani's 1997 confession was true or false, it was certainly convenient."

Gaertner/Wodele Affair

John Wodele (pronounced wood-lee)

John Wodele, post WWII baby, grew up in southern Minnesota, worked in his family's business and was a two-term mayor of Wabasha, Minnesota.

In 1985, the 38 year-old Wodele was summoned to work for his longtime friend, Ramsey County attorney Tom Foley. Foley had created a new position for Wodele as his spokesman and executive assistant. Wodele was needed to defuse the furor over Foley's alleged cover up or misdirection of Kathleen Greening's 1982 murder. Wodele would also help Foley advance his political ambitions and Foley was re-elected in 1986 and 1990.

In 1994 Foley gave up his job as county attorney to run for the U.S. Senate. He lost.

Gaertner ran for Foley's vacated job in 1994. She won. She was now the Ramsey County attorney.

After Gaertner took office she continued the corrupt practices she had learned since 1984. She created a new position for John Wodele as her chief of staff. A few years later, she selected him to be director of the Child Support Enforcement Division, and raised his salary from $58,750 to $90,000 per year. Then they had an affair. They would travel together extensively in 1995 and 1996.

Additional activities surrounding Wodele:

1980s: Wodele was associated with the Democratic
  Leadership Council. During this time he met
  Steven Bosacker, who would later become Jesse
  Ventura's chief of staff and get Wodele his present
  job as Ventura's communications director.

1992: Minnesota coordinator for Clinton's
  presidential campaign.

1993: Ran for mayor of Minneapolis and finished sixth.

1994: Wodele's boss Tom Foley decided not to run for
  re-election as county attorney in order to run for
  the U.S. Senate. He lost.

1994: Gaertner ran for election to Foley's job and won.

1995: Gaertner creates a new position for Wodele as
  her chief of staff.

1996: Gaertner appoints Wodele director of the Child
  Support Enforcement Division at $90,000/year.

1998: On September 9, Wodele resigned from his
  Gaertner-created job due to the publicity of his
  romantic relationship with his boss. Several
  months later he would get a job with Ventura.

During this time, Wodele also served on the
Minneapolis Planning Commission where he made
many incorrect decisions. His worst decision allowed
the destruction of five historic buildings on the
Mississippi riverfront, in order to make way for the
Federal Reserve Bank to build an office building.

Some time in the 1990s, Wodele and Gaertner began their affair. In 1995 and 1996 they traveled to meetings and conferences at county expense [of course, on important county business]. According to county records they visited Las Vegas, Phoenix, Nashville, Washington, D.C. and Naples, Florida.

In 1998, several "concerned employees" in the County Attorney's office complained to the Ramsey County Board of Commissioners that the Gaertner/Wodele relationship was having a negative impact on the Child Enforcement Division. The following is an excerpt from the "concerned employees" complaint about Wodele:

> "It is common knowledge in the division that John and Susan are sexually intimate. John was promoted to director of child support with no management or child support experience. Because he is involved personally and sexually with the county attorney his focus is on pleasing her so all the decisions about the division is compromised..."

> "John spends lots of time assisting Susan in non-child support duties. He is rarely in the office. He is on the board of many banks and attends their meetings. It is expected that he will spend lot of time assisting Susan in the campaign as he did the last election [1994]..."

> "John does not listen, talks too much and thinks he knows more than he does. He lacks the knowledge and skills to manage this office. He has not taken time to understand child

support enough to make knowledgeable decisions. Most staff have no respect for John or Susan and our office is compromised by their personal relationship."

The complaint closes with:

"It is time for the Public, the Commissioners, the County manager and others to be aware of what a devastating and unethical situation exists in our office."

On August 30, 1998, the *St. Paul Pioneer Press* reported that Gaertner and Wodele had been having an affair since at least early 1997. It also reported the complaints of the concerned employees.

On September 9, 1998, Wodele resigned his $90,000 job.

One week after Wodele resigned, Gaertner received the completed investigators report of the bribery complaints.

Under the law Gaertner was obligated to:

- Send the case to a grand jury that has subpoena power

- File misdemeanor charges against Barkley and Ventura, or

- Dismiss the complaints for no probable cause

She stalled and held the case.

On September 15, 1998, Ventura won his uncontested primary election and would now square off against his two main opponents: Coleman and Humphrey.

Ventura's popularity was rising in every poll. All indicators gave him a chance to be Minnesota's next governor. If Gaertner manipulated the case properly and Ventura became governor, she would be able to put Wodele back to work.

Gaertner knew from reading the investigator's report and listening to their taped interviews, that Barkley and Ventura were guilty of bribing Bill Dahn. When she read the transcript of Ventura being interviewed by Joe Soucheray on the day after the bribe, she couldn't help but be convinced that they broke the law. She knew they were guilty but she sat on the case.

Gaertner didn't have the honor or courage to do the right thing and charge Barkley and Ventura with misdemeanor crimes for victimizing Bill Dahn. Remember that Gaertner was weaned in the Ramsey County attorney's office, where ethics and honor were and still are, virtually non-existent.

Gaertner stalled the bribery complaints because she was up for re-election and she said that having Ventura in the race would improve her chances of winning. She was right.

On November 5, 1998, the *Star Tribune* quoted Gaertner, "I had no party endorsement, no special-interest group endorsement, no newspaper endorsement, I just had the endorsement of a majority of the people, and that is a good feeling. Me and Jesse."

In the same article Gaertner said, "I feel a kinship with a governor who broke all the political rules and defied the conventional wisdom, and took his case directly to the people."

Gaertner said the above while sitting on the completed investigators report.

Gaertner may try to argue that the case wasn't closed when the investigative report was filed on September 15, 1998 because Ole Savior, another gubernatorial candidate, met with investigator Hoff on November 4 and a meaningless memo was added to the file that supposedly kept it open.

Whatever she says would be irrelevant anyway because she had a conflict of interest from the moment she received the complaints.

Ole Savior, DFL gubernatorial candidate, filed a contested election case on November 10, 1998, in the Minnesota Supreme Court. Chief Justice Blatz should have ordered a three-judge panel to hear Savior's contested election case as required by law. Instead she took it upon herself to make the decision that Savior's complaint was not timely and she dismissed it. A clear violation of the law. The merits of Savior's case were not heard.

Savior filed another complaint and requested a restraining order to prevent Ventura's inauguration because he obtained the office by fraud. He filed it with Ramsey County District Court Chief Judge Lawrence Cohen. Cohen dismissed the case without a hearing and the merits of the case were never heard.

Savior has requested the United States Supreme Court to hear the constitutional issues related to his complaints.

The investigators didn't call Savior and as far as they were concerned, the investigation was complete when they filed their report on September 15, 1998.

On November 3, 1998, Ventura became governor and now Gaertner held all the cards.

On November 12, 1998, Wodele called governor-elect Ventura's chief of staff Bosacker and said, "if there's anything I can do to help, call me."

Gaertner used Wodele's call to Bosacker as an excuse to claim that she now had a conflict of interest. *Bull!* She had the conflict the day the complaints against Barkley arrived in her office in July 1998, because her boyfriend John Wodele and Dean Barkley were friends. Now, after waiting five months, she sent the bribery complaints to Anoka County on December 17 for a determination. *SURPRISE!* Anoka County? Where did I hear that name before?

Gaertner's former boss, Tom Foley, waited four years to claim a conflict of interest in the Greening murder case and then he sent it to Anoka County, also. In both cases, John Wodele and Charles Balck played significant roles by helping Foley and Gaertner.

Gaertner's office kept Barkley and Ventura's lawyers, Villaume and Heffelfinger, illegally informed about the status of the case. Did I say Heffelfinger? Where did I see that name before?

Charles Balck

Author's note: Assistant Ramsey County attorney Charles Balck was helping Gaertner manage the bribery case. I had a pretty good idea that he was helping strategize the stall and the fix, but I wanted to confirm my suspicions. So, I asked him a few questions.

I asked Balck, in a letter, why Anoka County was selected to determine the outcome of the Barkley/Ventura bribery case.

Balck answered, in a letter, "the fact that Anoka County was ultimately selected was just the luck of the draw."

In a follow-up letter I asked Balck, verbatim, how the "draw" was conducted:

• Do you use a lottery system?

• Do you select a county in a certain order?

• Are there any notes or paper work regarding which county would handle this case?

• Did your office send letters to various counties asking who had time to work on it?

• Who made the decision to send this case to Anoka County and why?

• Where is the documentation?

I also asked Balck when and why the bribery case was determined to be a conflict of interest for Ramsey County.

Balck answered by letter and on the phone that, "a staff member [John Wodele] of this office applied for and was under consideration for a position with Governor Ventura's administration."

I followed up and asked Balck, "if Wodele applied for a job with Governor Ventura it must have been after Ventura was elected in November. Then Wodele would not have been on your staff. If Wodele was not on your staff when Ventura was elected what would be the conflict of interest?"

I was not surprised when Balck answered, in a letter, "I decline to answer any further questions."

Bye, bye Balck.

Balck and others in the Ramsey County attorney's office kept Barkley informed about the bribery case against him. Barkley knew exactly what the Ramsey County attorney was doing at every step.

Barkley's team of lawyers, Thomas Heffelfinger and Phil Villaume, were kept informed by insiders at the Ramsey County attorney's office. They knew what was going on all the time. They helped develop and implement the plan that would have Anoka County dismiss the complaints. Anoka County? Where did I hear that name before?

Chapter Nine

Bribery Investigation

July 23 and 24, 1998,
two bribery complaints are filed.

September 15, bribery investigation
is completed and a report is filed.

December 17, Gaertner sends the
complaints to Anoka County.

December 28, Wodele is appointed
Ventura's communications director.

December 31, Anoka County James Weber
dismisses the complaints.

January 2, Charlie Weaver is appointed
Commissioner Department of Public Safety.

January 4, Ventura inauguration.

Bribery Complaint and Investigation Timeline

7/23   Dick Franson files a bribery complaint

7/24   Republican Party files a similar bribery complaint

7/30   Investigators Hoff and McNiff are assigned to investigate

8/6   Barkley interviewed and recorded by investigators

8/14   Dahn and Kane call investigators and decline to be interviewed

8/25   Friedline interviewed by investigators

9/3   Ventura interviewed by investigators

9/9   Wodele resigns Ramsey County job over affair with Susan Gaertner

9/15   Hoff submits completed Ramsey County investigative report

9/15   Ventura wins uncontested Reform Party primary election with 17,169 votes. Dahn receives 12,167 votes running as a Republican

11/3   Ventura wins the election for governor

11/3   Gaertner wins re-election for Ramsey County attorney

11/4   Ole Savior visits investigator Hoff, and Hoff adds memo to file

11/12   Wodele calls Ventura chief of staff Bosacker for a job

11/17   Weaver appointed to Ventura advisory committee

11/24   Heffelfinger takes affidavit from Dahn's running mate James Kane

12/07   Weaver goes pheasant hunting with Ventura

12/17   Gaertner sends complaints to Anoka County criminal prosecutor James Weber

12/28   Heffelfinger sends Kane's affidavit to Anoka County prosecutor James Weber

12/28   Wodele appointed Ventura communications director

12/31   Weber of Anoka County dismisses the complaints

1/2   Weaver appointed commissioner, Department of Public Safety

1/4   Ventura inauguration

1/7   Franson files complaint against Gaertner for stonewalling his complaint

2/4   Weber of Anoka County appointed to Commission on Judicial Selection

Part 1

By July 24, 1998, Dick Franson and the Minnesota Republican Party had filed complaints with Ramsey County attorney Susan Gaertner, alleging that Dean Barkley and Jesse Ventura bribed Bill Dahn to withdraw his candidacy in the Reform Party.

As soon as County attorney Gaertner received the complaints against Barkley she should have declared that she had a conflict of interest. Her boyfriend and employee John Wodele was connected to Barkley by virtue of the fact that he had received Barkley's Reform Party endorsement when he ran for mayor of Minneapolis in 1993. Barkley and Wodele were buddies and Gaertner knew it.

Ramsey County investigators Hoff and McNiff were assigned to investigate the complaints. They recorded interviews with Dean Barkley (August 6, 1998), Doug Friedline (August 25, 1998) and Jesse Ventura (September 3, 1998). Dahn and his running mate Kane, followed Barkley's instructions and refused to be interviewed.

At the close of Friedline's interview, investigator Hoff asked if he and the others had gotten together to go over what they would say when questioned because, "the stories are uniform past the point of what would be true." Friedline said they never met as a group and that he was a small part of the picture. Investigators asked Ventura the same question and Ventura said he "always tells the truth."

The investigators submitted their investigative report on September 15, 1998.

Excerpts from the recorded interviews are interspersed throughout this chapter.

Since Gaertner did not declare a conflict of interest when she received the completed investigative report on September 15, she was required by law (Minn. Stat. 211B.16) to either:

• **Charge Barkley and Ventura with misdemeanors**

• **Send the case to a grand jury that had subpoena power, or**

• **Dismiss the complaints for no probable cause**

Instead of following the law she did none of these. She stalled.

Gaertner would hold the case until December, declare she had a conflict of interest, and send the case to Anoka County for a decision. Gaertner had the conflict of interest in July when the complaints arrived in her office. The conflict was greater than the fact that boyfriend Wodele had asked Ventura's chief of staff for a job.

VENTURA - investigators asked Ventura if money was discussed at Dahn's home on July 19 and he said, "maybe a little." He then told the investigators that he didn't ask Dahn where he had gotten the money to register because it was none of his business.

BARKLEY - told the investigators the opposite. He said that when he and Ventura were at Dahn's home on July 19 Ventura DID ask Dahn where he got the $600 to register and Dahn told him he used his mortgage money.

Barkley told the investigators that when Ventura asked Dahn and Kane what they considered to be their party affiliation both men said they had always been Republicans and wanted to register as such on July 14, but were advised by a staff person at the Secretary of State's office that they could not.

Does Bill Dahn sound like a Republican? He's Native American, living on monthly disability income and is an advocate for the elderly. He's also an environmental activist, gets most of his food from a food shelf where he volunteers and eats many of his meals at a church, along with the poor and the elderly.

Barkley explained to investigators that he told Dahn and Kane that they either misunderstood the Secretary of State or were given erroneous information and that they could have registered as Republicans. Barkley said, "they became very upset and said they felt they were misled and they were going down to the Secretary of State's office the next week to correct the problem."

How could they correct the problem? Dahn had used his mortgage money to file the previous week and he didn't have anymore money. Even if he did have the money, why would he spend it to file again when he was already in the race? Dahn told the media he was happily registered in the Reform

Party. It was only the bribery and promises made by Ventura and Barkley that got him to switch to the Republican Party.

Investigator McNiff knew Barkley was lying about what he knew about Dahn's money situation. McNiff got firm and moved in on Barkley:

McNiff: If mortgage money was put up (initially), didn't that indicate that Dahn didn't have money? It never entered your mind that Dahn didn't have the money?

Barkley: I know the campaign laws.

McNiff: So when you left his house, were you not under the impression that they did not have a lot of money?

Barkley: I knew they didn't have a lot of money.

McNiff: So the next day you found out—.

Barkley: Two days later.

McNiff: Didn't that suggest that they didn't have more [money], since they had put up their mortgage money, wouldn't that be an indication to you that they didn't have any money?

Barkley: It could be.

McNiff: When you found out that they were not going to get their $600 refund—.

Barkley: I know the campaign laws. I got sick in his house.

Barkley was stumbling badly and fell back on the, "I got sick in his house" lie numerous times. Ventura would use that lie also to divert attention from himself to Dahn's house. They both tried to make it appear that they felt sorry for Dahn.

Ventura told the investigators that Mavis Huddle, his campaign secretary, told him that Dahn had called the campaign office numerous times in the past several months. Huddle said that Dahn seemed troubled and wanted to get help from Ventura. Ventura was busy and never returned his calls. Now that Dahn had registered in the Reform Party, Ventura had time to come over to his house on a Sunday afternoon and bring Barkley with him.

Ventura told investigators that when he was at Dahn's house the air inside was so bad that he told Dahn he should sleep in his garage. He and Barkley didn't get sick in Dahn's house…they were having a ball screwing Dahn. They must have laughed like crazy all the way home.

Ventura told the investigators that they got so sick in Dahn's house they had to finish their meeting outside.

However, a video taken in Dahn's house on July 19 clearly shows that the meeting ended in Dahn's living room with Dahn, Kane, Ventura and Barkley standing together, smiling, laughing and shaking hands. Ventura and Barkley were not sick. They were very happy.

The video recorded Ventura telling Dahn and Kane that, "we'll plan then, on Tuesday at 3 o'clock, you guys are gonna go over with Dean and switch to become Republicans. We're gonna switch you—we're gonna switch you to being Republicans. We'll switch you—you're gonna be Republicans now. All you gotta do is walk in there and say, 'I am a Republican.'"

The investigators completed a 10 page written INVESTIGATIVE SUMMARY and submitted it to Susan Gaertner on September 15, 1998.

September 15, 1998, was primary election day. Ventura, running with no opposition, won the Reform primary with 17,169 votes. Dahn, running as a Republican against two others, received 12,167 votes and lost. Ventura would go to the general election in November and Dahn would go to the dump.

Gaertner would break the law again and again, as Foley and Wodele taught her, by stalling the case until well after she won reelection as Ramsey County attorney and Ventura won his election as governor.

She didn't have the guts or the character to send the case to a grand jury where it belonged because she knew it would cook Ventura and ruin any chance she had to get Wodele back on the public payroll. You will recall that Wodele and Gaertner's romantic relationship forced Wodele to resign on September 9, 1998.

Then, on December 17, 1998, five months after the complaints were filed and her boyfriend was assured a position in the Ventura administration, Gaertner sent the case to Anoka County for a determination. She claimed that she had a conflict of interest because Wodele sought a job with Governor Ventura.

Barkley knew the minute-by-minute status of the case because he was being kept informed from inside the Ramsey County attorney's office. There is evidence that attorneys Villaume and Heffelfinger knew the case was going to Weber in Anoka County. On December 28, 1998, Heffelfinger sent a fax with new information to Weber. But how did Heffelfinger know that Weber had the case?

It would be stupid to think that Gaertner, Balck, Wodele, Barkley, Villaume, Heffelfinger and Ventura would hold the case for five months and then let it go someplace that would not give them the "no probable cause" result they wanted. They knew they could count on Anoka County to help them out. They knew that James Weber, Anoka chief criminal prosecutor would get the case and clear them.

JUST TO BE CERTAIN, Barkley made sure that Weber got an appointment to the Commission on Judicial Selection, that the next judge from his district would be an existing or former employee of the Anoka County attorney's office and that he, Weber, would have influence in the Ventura administration… if he did the right thing.

But Barkley's biggest coup was getting Charlie Weaver on board. Weaver was a former Anoka County prosecutor and friend of Weber's. Weaver had just lost the election for attorney general and was now unemployed. Barkley got Weaver appointed to Ventura's advisory committee, arranged for Weaver to go hunting with Ventura on December 7, 1998, and then encouraged Ventura to appoint Weaver to the position of commissioner, Department of Public Safety.

Soon after the election Dahn was spinning out of control and Barkley was worried. Try as he may, Barkley couldn't get Dahn's house fixed as he promised. Dahn was screaming that he was double crossed by Barkley and Ventura.

Barkley called Dahn and left the following message on his voice mail: "I've been hearing stuff that you're dissatisfied with the effort we're trying to put in to help you. But I also have to keep a distance from you while the investigation is going on so the investigators don't try to say I'm trying to use some undue influence on you. So I've got some parameters that I've got to deal with legally and that's why I've had Phil (Madsen) and some other people from the staff gather the information so that we can come in and figure out what avenues of attack we have to do to get your house fixed."

Barkley was also concerned about investigator Hoff's report, because it included the transcript of Joe Soucheray's radio broadcast in which Ventura admitted he "bought off" Dahn. In addition, Barkley commented to the *Star Tribune*, July 22, 1998, that he wrote a check for Dahn to register as a Republican so Ventura would not have an opponent that could "knock Jesse off the air" by invoking federal equal-time broadcast rules. If these, and other comments were put together it would get harder and harder to fix the outcome. It didn't look good. They had to totally count on the boys up in Anoka County to come through for them.

Barkley knew that the evidence against him was piling up and would be difficult to overcome. He knew that Weber would do the right thing but he needed something fresh. Barkley got him Kane's affidavit. Weber relied upon it when he made his finding of no probable cause against Ventura and Barkley.

KANE AFFIDAVIT

James Kane
From video shot at Dahn's house, July 19.

Barkley frightened James Kane, former lieutenant governor candidate, into providing an affidavit that would be used by Weber to make his findings. Barkley told Kane that Dahn was out of control and he could bring them all down. The Kane affidavit was designed to support the lies told by Ventura and Barkley about the circumstances surrounding the July bribes.

Kane gave the affidavit to attorney Thomas Heffelfinger (Barkley and Ventura's attorney), on November 24, 1998, in a restaurant in Stillwater, Minnesota. Present at the taking of Kane's handwritten, six-page affidavit were attorney

Heffelfinger, private investigator and public notary James Molnar (hired by Heffelfinger to notarize the affidavit in the restaurant) and Kane's son.

Heffelfinger held onto Kane's affidavit until attorney Phil Villaume—Barkley's brother-in-law and Ventura's counsel—told him to fax it to Weber in Anoka County on December 28, 1998. This flurry of activity right near the end of a very busy December should have made Weber suspicious, unless for some reason he was looking the other way.

Weber had no way of knowing that Kane's affidavit was false. However, he should have suspected something was improper when he received it by fax from Heffelfinger, upon the instructions of Phil Villaume, and not from Ramsey County.

Why wasn't the Kane affidavit included when Gaertner sent the case to Anoka? Because she didn't have it. Heffelfinger had it. How did Villaume know that Anoka County had the case so he could tell Heffelfinger where and when to send the affidavit? Villaume knew what was going on because he was illegally and improperly kept informed by Barkley, Wodele and others.

Dick Franson, one of those who filed a bribery complaint, tried to get information about the status of the case. He was told that because it was an ongoing investigation, no one outside the Ramsey County attorney's office could know its status.

A major lie in Kane's affidavit, one that Weber relied upon, was that he and Dahn had more than $700 in cash with them at the Secretary of State's office when Barkley paid the $600 for them to register as Republicans. Kane wouldn't bring that amount of cash with him even if he had it, because the deal was that Barkley would pay any money that would be necessary.

When I questioned Weber in the hallway of his office in detail about this specific item, he became belligerent and refused to answer any further questions.

It is not believable that Weber would not have been suspicious of the rush job he was given on complaints that were more than five months old. However, Barkley and company wanted the matter settled before the January 4 inauguration and the Weaver appointment.

CHARLIE WEAVER

November 3, 1998: Charlie Weaver had just lost the election for state attorney general.

Weaver was now unemployed, uncertain about his future and he said he was going to take a vacation with his wife Julie and "talk matters over." (*Anoka County Union*)

Suddenly, Dean Barkley called and offered Weaver a position on Ventura's advisory committee. Weaver accepted and Ventura appointed him on November 17, 1998.

Weaver would later tell the *Anoka County Union* (December 18, 1998), "Dean Barkley called me after the election and asked me if I was interested. I thought about it for a while and I said, 'Sure…I want Jesse to be successful.'"

The *Anoka County Union* asked Weaver, "could the advisory committee post turn into something more permanent?" Weaver replied, "I think it's possible, but it's probably unlikely."

Prior to losing the election for attorney general, Weaver was a Republican State legislator for 10 years. He is anti-abortion, anti-marijuana and disliked Ventura's position on social issues. Weaver supported Republican Norm Coleman for governor over Ventura.

More importantly, Weaver was a former Anoka County criminal prosecutor and a friend of James Weber, chief attorney in the Criminal Division of Anoka County who would review the case.

On December 31, 1998, Weber rendered a decision dismissing the bribery charges against Ventura and Barkley.

On New Years weekend, two days after Weber's dismissal of the bribery case against Ventura and Barkley, the unemployed Weaver, a man with no organizational or executive experience, was appointed to a $97,300 per year job as the commissioner, Department of Public Safety, a department with nearly 2000 employees and a budget of more than $250 million.

In Weber's findings, he said there was no probable cause to charge Barkley and Ventura with crimes. He further said, "the facts and the allegations which form the basis for the complaints in this case were known and raised during the election campaign and received a fair amount of media attention."

He goes on to say that the allegations, "were therefore presumably known, and considered, by the electorate in voting in this election."

Weber is wrong. Crimes were committed by Ventura and Barkley, and Weber covered it up with verbose gibberish.

Chapter Ten

Conflict of Interest

Part 1

The law.

Minnesota Statute 43A.38, Subdivision 5 (a). Conflicts of interest.

> "use or attempted use of the employee's official position to secure benefits, privileges, exemptions or advantages for the employee or the employee's immediate family or an organization with which the employee is associated which are different from those available to the general public."

When Ventura did his wrestling referee gig on August 22, 1999, he violated 43A.38. It's clear that if he were not governor the World Wrestling Federation (WWF) would not have been interested in having the washed-up Ventura work for them.

On July 30, 1999, Minnesota ethics officer Sandra Hyllengren, met with Ventura's top aides to discuss Ventura's extracurricular activities. On August 2, 1999 she sent a memo to Bosacker, Wodele, Drewry and Brown stating:

> "According to the payroll division of DOER (Department of Employee Relations) the Governor is an employee who serves in the unclassified service...unclassified employees include those 'chosen by election or appointed to fill an elective office.' I can think of no easy way he can avoid being characterized as an employee given that inclusive language."

Hyllengren stated further that:

> "We discussed whether his newfound notoriety as Governor directly or indirectly affected book sales or the price he negotiated for the upcoming wrestling event. The statute prohibits use of the employee's official position to secure benefits...or advantages...which are different from those available to the general public. It further prohibits the use of 'prestige or influence of state office' for private gain. **Again I find it difficult, if not impossible, to stretch the plain meaning of the statute to the extent that I can justify ignoring an obvious conflict."**

On January 15, 1999, Alan Gilbert, chief deputy and solicitor general for the attorney general's office, sent a memo to Steven Bosacker, Ventura chief of staff. In it he stated:

"The governor and lieutenant governor appear
to be executive branch employees within the
meaning of chapter 43A. Indeed, an employee
is defined…to include 'any person currently
occupying or on leave from, a civil service
position.' This includes both classified and
unclassified positions, and thus applies to the
governor and lieutenant governor."

The only person who disagrees with the above
analysis is Julien Carter, commissioner of the
Department of Employee Relations. Carter was
brought in from Jefferson City, Missouri to take
Karen Carpenter's job. Carpenter was formerly
appointed by Governor Carlson, and Ventura kept
her on after praising her highly. When Carpenter
wouldn't play ball with the slime in Ventura's office,
the longtime state employee resigned. Actually, she
was driven out of office by the likes of Bosacker and
Wodele. They are as sick a pair as one could find
anywhere on the planet.

Part 2

When Ventura wanted to use the notoriety of the
governor's office, I went to court to stop him.

Ramsey County District Court judge Kathleen Gearin
ruled that I did not have standing as a private citizen
to bring the lawsuit against Ventura under statute 43A.
The statute allows a government agency or the
legislature to bring an action under 43A, but not a
private citizen like myself. She dismissed my case.
Actually she should have never heard the case because
of the standing issue. Why waste the court's time?

In her ORDER, Gearin, in addition to a lot of meaningless personal opinion gibberish, said, "THE COURT HAS A SERIOUS QUESTION REGARDING WHETHER THE GOVERNOR OF THE STATE OF MINNESOTA IS AN EMPLOYEE. THAT ISSUE IS NOT DECIDED TODAY.

Ventura's employee status was what my complaint was all about. That's what I went to court for.

Ventura and his insiders—Bosacker, Wodele and Drewry—spun what the judge said and the media chanted that story without coming back to me for a chance to rebut what they were saying. They said the judge found for Ventura and cleared the way for his outside activities. SHE DID NOT. She dismissed the case and made some personal ridiculous remarks.

Almost a year later,Ventura called me aside at the end of a meeting in a high school, where his moronic support for light rail was being discussed, and sarcastically thanked me for clearing the way for him to make as much money as he could— referring, of course, to Gearin's remarks.

Part 3

After his inauguration in January 1999, Ventura was in the national spotlight almost daily. This resulted in numerous offers for personal appearances. One of the offers was to referee a wrestling event called SummerSlam, scheduled for August 22, 1998, at the Target Center arena in Minneapolis.

Vince McMahon, president of the World Wrestling
Federation (WWF) gave Ventura a $100,000 advance
and a percentage of the pay-per-view revenue, to
referee at the SummerSlam event. Ventura gave the
$100,000 to charity and refused to disclose the
amount of money he would receive from the
pay-per-view audience. Some experts estimated
his income from that would be from one to two
million dollars.

It was common knowledge in the entertainment
world that Ventura had a running feud with WWF's
McMahon. McMahon had used Ventura's name and
likeness without permission. Ventura sued McMahon
and won a settlement in excess of $800,000.

Some of the questions being asked were:

• Why would the WWF want to hire Ventura when he
  had sued them successfully?

• Why would it be improper for Ventura to take the
  job if he did it on his time off?

The WWF knew the publicity value of having the
now-famous governor referee the event. There is no
dispute that if Ventura had not been elected governor,
McMahon would have snubbed him.

Ventura would say *it's Sunday night and my own
personal time. Even a judge said it was okay for me to do it.*
Ventura would use the judge's gibberish time and time
again to deceive the public.

SOME PEOPLE SAID:

SO WHAT? WHAT'S THE BIG DEAL?

HE'S ONLY BEING JESSE.

The big deal is that when Ventura came into office in 1999, Minnesota was flush with cash and the future looked great. He was so busy looking for work elsewhere that he ignored the needs of the state and concentrated on becoming a multi-millionaire while jobs dried up and Minnesota became a debtor state. THAT'S THE BIG DEAL.

Part 4

My case in court related specifically to whether Ventura violated the state "conflict of interest law" by participating as a referee in a World Wrestling Federation event in Minneapolis on August 22, 1999.

State law prohibits employees from using their position for their personal financial gain.

When Ventura was inaugurated in January 1999 he became an "employee" of the State and subject to the State laws, which prohibit "employees" from using their "official position to secure benefits…which are different from those available to the general public."

Jesse Ventura is the duly elected governor of Minnesota and as such he is an employee of the State and subject to the laws that relate to employees. It is a violation of Minnesota law for State employees to use their office for personal financial gain.

Some people think it's okay for the governor to take whatever outside employment he wants, whenever he wants, but that is not so.

In 1999, when I challenged Ventura's SummerSlam activity in court, he argued that he was not an employee of the state and was not using his office for his personal financial gain. He was just doing some work on his private time.

Yet in Michael Uschan's 2001 book about Jesse Ventura, *People in the News* (Lucent Books, page 83), there was a discussion about Ventura using his office as governor to make money for himself and Ventura finally admitted:

"I'm entrepreneuring myself," the governor says. "Jesse Ventura is my product. I am able to sell Jesse Ventura as the commodity he is." Ventura admitted that holding the State's highest elected office helped him personally. "I'm sure it has," he says. "Anyone would be lying to say it didn't."

The SummerSlam event in Minnesota was available to Ventura only because he was elected governor and received national notoriety. Prior to being elected governor McMahon and Ventura were enemies and McMahon was conspicuously absent from Ventura's inauguration.

At the SummerSlam event Ventura said, "as long as you're in this State, you hold no power here. It's very simple. It's the Body Rules. It's my rules or the highway." —*To Dane Smith*, Star Tribune, *July 15, 1999*

He probably meant to say, "My way or the highway."

By entering into the arrangement and appearing for the WWF, Ventura violated the law because he clearly used his "official position to secure benefits...which are different from those available to the general public," which are prohibited by statute.

As a constitutional officer in the State of Minnesota, the governor is an officer within the executive branch and since he is an officer within the executive branch he is considered an employee.

The State Legislature should have rallied around my fight, but so many of them have so many special interest conflicts, that they were scared. So they stuck their heads in the sand.

Chapter Eleven

Military Career

Ventura **WAS NOT A NAVY SEAL**
while on active duty.

Ventura **WAS NOT A NAVY SEAL**
during the Vietnam war.

Ventura **WAS NOT IN COMBAT**
in Vietnam.

This chapter is not intended to demean Ventura's military service or his claims of countless visits to various whorehouses and bars throughout Asia, California and Nevada while in the service of his country.

Several people were contacted for this chapter. Two of them are included in this book:

• Bill Salisbury, U.S. Navy SEAL Commanding Officer (retired)

• Dick Franson, U.S. Army Master Sergeant (retired)

Part 1

On December 14, 1999, Minnesota Public Radio (MPR) interviewed John Wodele, professional liar and Ventura communications director. Wodele assured listeners that Ventura never tried to mislead reporters or the public, and that he has been careful to equivocate whenever referring to himself as a SEAL (SEa Air and Land).

Wodele also confirmed that Ventura was in the UDTs (Underwater Demolition Team), and he said the governor had never tried to convince people otherwise. In fact, Wodele said, "he corrected me in the past [when referring to him as a SEAL]."

Two weeks after Wodele's interview with Minnesota Public Radio, *Rolling Stone* Magazine published the following Ventura quote [December 30, 1999]: "I was in the SEALs during the Vietnam War, so I experienced firsthand how we, as Americans, were affected by that conflict."

Six months prior to Wodele's comments on MPR Ventura appeared on Larry King Live, June 3, 1999.

Larry King: "You were a Navy SEAL?"

Jesse Ventura: "Yes."

King: "What was that like?"

Ventura: "Exciting. I did it at 18 years old to 22, 22 and-a-half. It was challenging. I would belong to no other unit. The camaraderie is unbelievable."

Ventura lied constantly about being a SEAL while on active duty. In all of Ventura's quotes in this chapter, he refers to himself as a SEAL. He never mentions the honorable UDT organization that he was actually a member of.

Retired commander Bill Salisbury spent 16 years as a Navy SEAL from 1967 until his retirement in 1983. He was officer-in-charge of SEAL Team ONE Detachment GOLF in Vietnam, executive officer of SEAL Team TWO during the war and commanding officer of Underwater Demolition Team ELEVEN. Prior to becoming a SEAL, Commander Salisbury was a naval gunfire spotter and liaison officer for the U.S. Marines. He served one tour in Vietnam with the Marines in I Corps. Commander Salisbury now practices law in San Diego, California.

Navy SEAL Commander Bill Salisbury (retired)

UDTs and SEALs all undergo Basic Underwater Demolition/SEAL training (BUD/S). To his credit, Ventura completed BUD/S very rigorous training.

Salisbury explains the difference between UDTs (Underwater Demolition Team) and SEALs (SEa Air and Land).

Said Salisbury, "To earn the right to call himself a 'SEAL,' a man had to serve in a SEAL rather than [in] an Underwater Demolition Team for at least six months and be recommended for the SEAL classification 5326 by his commanding officer. Such classification would appear on the man's DD 214 discharge certificate. The 5326 designation does not appear on Ventura's DD 214 only the 5321/22 designation for Underwater Demolition. Ventura was not even 'technically' a SEAL, even though he served a very short time with a reserve UDT/SEAL unit. He was never awarded the 5326 classification.

Salisbury (far left) with some *real* SEALs.

"UDTs had the mission of beach reconnaissance in advance of Marine amphibious landings, while SEALs were tasked with counter-guerrilla operations in Vietnam that included ambushes, prisoner of war recovery and abduction or assassination of enemy political cadre. UDT was joined at the hip with Marines aboard ships at sea; SEALs had nothing to do with Marines and fought from bases within Vietnam. Reflecting these differing missions, SEAL Team One had 34 men killed in Vietnam while UDT 12, Ventura's outfit, lost but a single man and that was two years before Ventura joined the team. UDT 12 lost no men during Ventura's time in the Western Pacific."

Commander Salisbury calls Ventura a "phony SEAL."

There are quite a few "phony SEALs" but none as notorious as Ventura. While some former SEALs endorse Ventura calling himself a SEAL, most do not. Those agreeing with Ventura are simply kowtowing to his celebrity.

The author on military maneuvers.
Fort Ord military reservation, in California.

Author note: A multi-medalled Vietnam veteran, scheduled for this location in the book, cancelled out at the last minute for political reasons. I reluctantly substituted for him to fill the space. I hope you enjoy my picture, taken around the time Ventura was likely entering kindergarten.

Part 2

Ventura is a Vietnam era veteran and he received the Vietnam veteran's bonus. (He also received government money to go to Hennepin Community College in the early 1970s. Now he tells students that they shouldn't expect the government to help them pay for their schooling.)

When Ventura wasn't in the bars and whorehouses of the Philippines, or playing football, he served on board a ship as a storeroom clerk. His ship likely passed close enough to the Vietnam coastline to qualify him for the Vietnam veteran's bonus.

In July 1998, Dick Franson was the first person to disclose that Ventura was not a Navy SEAL during the Vietnam war, and that Ventura did not see combat while in the military.

Dick Franson
is a highly decorated U.S. Army Master Sergeant (ret.)
who served with distinction in Korea and Vietnam.

On December 1, 1998, the *GLOBE* newspaper reported
that Franson said, "I think he [Ventura] inflated his
record to pump up his tough guy image...I knew cooks
who saw more action..."

"It just makes me sick," fumes Franson. "You don't
mislead the public about something like that. You
don't stretch your military record too far to make
people think you did more than you did."

The *GLOBE* reported that Ventura received the
Vietnam Service Medal and the National Defense
Service Medal. Franson pooh-poohed the Vietnam
Service Medal. He said, "I think it's very strange that
all Jesse has to show for his supposed time over there
is a Vietnam Service Medal, for which you only need
one day in the country or on a ship 20 miles or less out
to sea. If he [Ventura] cruised past the coastline one
day, he was eligible for that award."

Franson said that Ventura's National Defense Service
Medal is given to all military personnel who complete
basic training.

Franson was the first to report that Ventura DOES
NOT HAVE the Combat Action Ribbon. Ventura also
DOES NOT HAVE the Vietnam Campaign Medal,
which is for those who served six months or longer in
Vietnam.

About the Combat Action Ribbon

SEAL Commander Salisbury writes that, "any
member of the Navy who engaged the enemy
during the Vietnam War in a ground action often
referred to as a 'firefight' qualified for and would
have been awarded a Combat Action Ribbon. The
Navy would also have awarded the ribbon to any
member who was in an area where a firefight was
likely. Lack of a Combat Action Ribbon, therefore,
signifies that a sailor such as Jim Janos [Ventura]
never was in a firefight or served in an area where
he would likely engage in a firefight." This Salisbury
statement was published by cursor.org.

Ventura told the *GLOBE* that he, "went on missions behind enemy lines in Vietnam that would make his political opponents wet their pants."

When Ventura was questioned about why he does not have the Combat Action Ribbon, he said, "to the best of my knowledge I was never fired upon." According to Salisbury, "he didn't have to be 'fired upon' to get the Combat Action Ribbon. He just had to be near the action." As a storeroom clerk, it is unlikely that Ventura would have been "fired upon" unless a gunman robbed the store.

"To the best of my knowledge I was never fired upon." —*Ventura to the* St. Paul Pioneer Press, *January 28, 2002.*

Ventura used similar obfuscating language with investigators who were interviewing him for bullying and bribing Bill Dahn. When he was cornered in his lies, Ventura would tell the investigators, "I don't recall" or "I can't think for other people."

He told the investigators that he always tells the truth. As an example of his honesty, and to divert attention from his crime, he told investigators a stupid story about a time he was in Rochester, Minnesota during the 1998 campaign. He was in a debate with Humphrey and Coleman when a woman handed him a piece of paper and a pencil so he could take notes. He rejected her offer, claiming that he didn't need notes since he always tells the truth. Maybe if he took some notes, Minnesota wouldn't have gone from a wealthy state to a debtor state.

Part 3

Ventura Quotes About Being a SEAL

Ventura lets interviewers refer to him as a Navy SEAL, or an ex-Navy SEAL, which they routinely do without correcting him. He also consistently refers to himself as a SEAL, without explaining the distinctions between SEALs and UDTs. Nowhere in the complete text or transcripts of the various articles, interviews or television and radio programs, are the words Underwater Demolition Team, or the acronym UDT, ever mentioned.

Navy SEAL, union member, volunteer high school football coach, outdoorsman, husband of 23 years, father of two. —*Ventura Campaign Advertisement*

"I'm a warrior at heart. I'm an ex-Navy SEAL."
—The New York Times, *October 31, 1998*

"And Mr. [Hulk] Hogan, I mean he wants to be me, anyway. He always—you know, he pretends to be a Navy SEAL; I was one."
—*Meet the Press, November 8, 1998*

"You know, I come from a little bit of a military background earlier in my life and we were always taught in the Navy SEAL team never to assume."
—CNN *Inside Politics, November 12, 1998*

High Times: "Was your wrestling career fun?"
Ventura: "It was exciting. And for me, an ex-Navy Seal, it was fun."
—High Times *Magazine, November 1998*

Ventura: "I've been a Navy SEAL."
Maria Shriver: "But, a Navy SEAL makes you ready to be governor?"
Ventura: "Uh-huh. Yeah. Sure it does."
Maria Shriver: "Where did you come up with that?"
Ventura: "It's easy—because I defy—because I worked with things in being a Navy SEAL that could kill me."
—NBC Dateline, December 22, 1998

"I'm the top law enforcement officer in the state of Minnesota. I'm also the commander-in-chief of the National Guard. I'm an ex-Navy SEAL team member."
—Meet The Press, February 21, 1999

"Now as a Navy SEAL, I thought, how did they know that about me—how dangerous we truly can be? We have a saying in the SEALs: we don't get mad, we get even."
—National Press Club Speech, February 22, 1999

"I'm the head of the state troopers, and the commander-in-chief of the National Guard. I'm also a former Navy SEAL."
—CNN Late Edition, February 23, 1999

Tim Russert: "Both your brother-your older brother and yourself, [were] Navy SEALs?"
Ventura: "Mm-hmm, yeah."
Tim Russert: "You almost died twice, once as a Navy SEAL and once as a wrestler, with blood clots in your lungs."
Ventura: "Well, I almost died more than that a couple times as a SEAL."
—Tim Russert Show, May 22, 1999

"I rappelled down from the top of the Target Center before a Timberwolves [Minnesota professional basketball team] game. But, you know, I am an ex-Navy SEAL and I was trained for you know, a full year and was very comfortable in that type of rappelling-type thing."
—*Larry King Live, May 24, 1999*

"I couldn't care less what a person's sexual orientation is, and I'm an ex-Navy SEAL."
—The Advocate, *May 1999*

"First of all, they should understand why a Navy SEAL doesn't wear underwear."
—*CBS This Morning, June 3, 1999*

Larry King: "You were a Navy SEAL?"
Jesse Ventura: "Yes."
King: "What was that like?"
Ventura: "Exciting. I did it at 18 years old to 22, 22 and a half. It was challenging. I would belong to no other unit. The camaraderie is unbelievable."
—*Larry King Live, June 3, 1999*

"When I was a wrestler, I could pick up buildings. When I was a SEAL, I could scale them."
—*NPR's Fresh Air, June 3, 1999*

Chris Matthews: "When you were a—you were a SEAL, you must have been through amazingly scary moments with life and death."
Ventura: "Mm-hmm. Yeah."
—*Hardball with Chris Matthews at Harvard University, October 6, 1999*

"You're talking to an ex-Navy Seal here."
—*Ventura in* Playboy, *November 1999.*

"I was in the SEALs during the Vietnam War, so I experienced firsthand how we, as Americans, were affected by that conflict."
—Rolling Stone *Magazine, December 30, 1999*

"We're a proud organization. If anyone tries to pretend they're a SEAL, God help them."
—*Jesse Ventura Autobiography,* I Ain't Got Time to Bleed

Always Cheat!

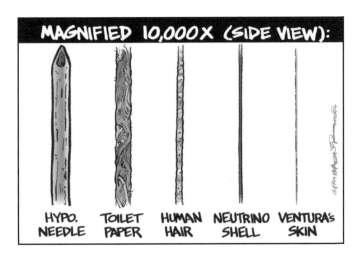

Chapter Twelve

Ventura Quotes

AFTER THOUGHTFUL RECONSIDERATION, GOVERNOR VENTURA DECIDES NOT TO PROMOTE HIS BOOK ON THE HOWARD STERN SHOW

The collection of quotes in this chapter provide a clear picture of just how insulting, nasty and inconsiderate Ventura really is.

Upon Ventura's ascension into the office of governor, he became a multi-millionaire and Minnesota went from being a wealthy state to a debtor state.

Jesse Ventura is a threat who should not be discounted. He is rude and intolerant.

He insults those who disagree with him and considers himself beyond reproach, untouchable, a self-professed king.

When Ventura is challenged about his insults he tells people to, "lighten up. I was only kidding." *Joke, joke, joke. Can't you take a joke? Ha, ha, ha.*

Because Ventura acts like a buffoon, many people let him get away with insults, apologies then more insults. A vicious circle.

VENTURA STATEMENTS - alphabetical by category

BRAIN

> "My brain is operating at such a level that I don't want to put my foot in it."
> —*To Matt Bai and David Brauer,* Newsweek, *11/16/98*

COOL

"I am cool. Mentally, I'm still 21 or 22 in a lot of ways."
—*To Matt Bai and David Brauer*, Newsweek, *11/16/98*

FLAG

"If you buy the flag it's yours to burn."
—*To Lawrence Grobel*, Playboy, *11/99*

GOOD LOOKING

"When I get up in the morning, all I have to do is brush my teeth and know how good looking I am."
—*To Bob Von Sternberg, startribune.com, 11/18/98*

GOVERNMENT (Ventura Supports Mandatory Seat Belt Laws)

"Ladies and gentlemen, you cannot legislate stupidity. People are going to do stupid things. We cannot sit and every time someone does something stupid, make it a law and have the government come in, because if you do that, you're going to lose your freedoms."
—*To Paul Gray*, Time *Magazine*

HONESTY (Regarding President Clinton)

"When he lied to me like that he will never have credibility again. I will think, 'is he telling me the truth or is he giving me a line of b.s.?'"
—*To wcco.com, 2/12/99*

HONESTY 2

"My fault is honesty. When I'm asked a question, I give an honest answer."
—*To Robert Whereatt, Conrad deFiebre, Dane Smith,* Star Tribune, *10/1/99*

HUNTING

"Ventura and company went pheasant hunting at Wild Wings game farm in Hugo, Minnesota on December 7, 1998."
—*Reported by Debra O'Connor,* St. Paul Pioneer Press, *12/8/98*

HUNTING 2

"Until you've hunted man, you haven't hunted yet. Because you need to hunt something that can shoot back at you to really classify yourself as a hunter. You need to understand the feeling of what it's like to go into the field and know your opposition can take you out. Not just go out there and shoot Bambi."
—*To Chris Niskanen,* St. Paul Pioneer Press, *4/6/01*

INDIAN TREATY RIGHTS

"If those rules apply, then they ought to be back in birch-bark canoes instead of 200-horsepower Yamaha engines with fish finders. Then it comes back to this: How can one person be allowed to do this and another can't?"
—*To wcco.com, 1999*

JUDGMENT

"Judge me by my policies, judge me by me commissioners and judge me by the work that we're trying to do, not a feeding frenzy of media so you can get ratings and make money."
—*To cnn.com, 10/5/99*

KING

"It's good to be the king. The best thing is that there's no one in this state who can tell me what to do."
—*To Lawrence Grobel,* Playboy, *11/99*

LINGERIE

"If I could be reincarnated as a fabric, I would like to come back as a 38 double-D bra."
—*To Lawrence Grobel,* Playboy, *11/99*

LIVING IT UP

"I'm having the time of my life right now! It's nice—when you're governor, you can kind of dictate your own way. I can walk around now and say, 'Jump!' and there are four people who say, 'how high?'"
—*To* City Pages, *12/2/98*

MEDIA

"I enjoy my relationship with the media, I really do. Because I'm a warrior. And I'm at an age now when I can't go out and be a warrior, so I have to be a mental one. So I've chosen you to be my adversaries."
—*To Steve Dornfeld*, Minnesota Law and Politics, *11/99*

MILITARY

"Just outside the main gate [Subic Bay] was a mile of road that held something like 350 bars and ten thousand girls, and that was every night. Imagine being nineteen, maybe closing in on twenty, and in the best physical shape of your life. We went out bar-hopping every night."
—*In* Ain't Got Time To Bleed, *by Jesse Ventura*

MINDSPEAK

"I'm not afraid to speak my mind. If I don't get re-elected that's fine. I'll go back to the private sector from whence I came."
—*To Jean McMillan, cnn.com, 10/7/99*

MONEY

"When there's money involved there ain't no friends."
—*To David Hanners*, St. Paul Pioneer Press, *10/19/98*

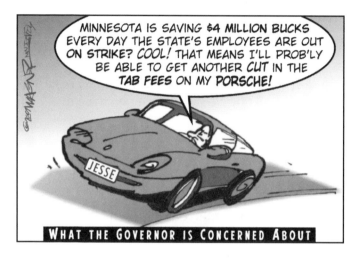

MOTHERS

"I don't want to seem hard-core, but why did you become a parent? It takes two people to parent. Is it the government's job to make up for someone's mistake?"
—*Neal*

NEW YORKERS

"Coleman? This is a New Yorker, you remember. He thinks milk comes from a carton. He's never even seen a cow."
—*To wcco.com, 8/9/8, regarding St. Paul, MN mayor Norm Coleman*

PHILOSOPHY

"Win if you can, lose if you must, but ALWAYS CHEAT."
—*1998 speech to University of Minnesota students*

PHILOSOPHY 2

"Admit nothing, deny everything, make counter accusations."
—*To David Letterman on Late Night with David Letterman*

PRESIDENT

"Who knows, you know? Four years as mayor, then maybe governor, maybe senator or maybe, at the year 2000, Jesse The Body in the White House. Be something to think about."
—*To Pat Doyle, Mike Kaszuba,* Star Tribune, *1/10/99*

PRESIDENT

"I promised I wouldn't run for president. I never said nothing about the V.P."
—*To Dane Smith,* Star Tribune, *5/19/99*

RADIO

"It's my show and I can do what I want. Who said
I had to be responsible?"
—*To Jake Tapper*, Body Slam, *1999*

REFEREE

"As long as you're in this state, you hold no power
here. It's very simple. It's the Body Rules. It's my
rules or the highway."
—*To Dane Smith*, Star Tribune, *7/15/99*

REFEREE 2

"You're in my state now, I am law and order here."
—*www.venturafiles.com 8/22/99*

RELIGION

"Organized religion is a sham and a crutch for
weak-minded people who need strength in
numbers. It tells people to go out and stick their
noses in other people's business."
—*To Lawrence Grobel*, Playboy, *11/99*

ST. PAUL, MN IRISH

"Minneapolis. Well I was born in Minneapolis.
And, besides, have you ever been to St. Paul?
Whoever designed the streets must have been
drunk...In St. Paul, there's no rhyme nor reason. It's
not numerical. It's not alphabetical. I think it was
those Irish guys, you know what they like to do."
—*To wcco.com, 2/24/99*

SEAL

"I operate under a rule I learned during my SEALs training: Keep it simple and stupid."
—*To Lawrence Grobel,* Playboy, *11/99*

SHUT UP

"So for all those naysayers out there who say, 'Oh, the governor shouldn't be standing in front of the cameras, the governor shouldn't be bringing attention to himself,' and all of the stuff that I get, all the crap from the people that don't like me out there-well, this is in your face now, because you all can shut up."
—*To Dane Smith,* Star Tribune, *6/26/99*

STUDENT HELP FOR COLLEGE

"You don't need the government. There are plenty of ways to get through college. You're smart enough."
—*To Mary Jane Smetanka,* Star Tribune, *11/18/98*

(The government paid for Ventura to go to N. Hennepin Community College in 1974.)

SUICIDE

"If you're to the point of killing yourself, and you're that depressed, life can only get better. If you're a feeble weak-minded person to begin with, I don't have time for you."
—*Lawrence Grobel*, Playboy, *11/99*

VIRGINITY

"The girl was older than me and she wasn't a virgin. So who got seduced?"
—*In* Ain't' Got Time To Bleed, *by Jesse Ventura*

WIFE

On ABC-TV, October 8, 1999, Ventura told Barbara Walters that his wife was "weak-minded" for being an adherent of organized religion and suggested that he has told her as much.
—*Reported by Conrad deFiebre and Noel Holston,* Star Tribune, *10/9/99*

ADDITIONAL FACTS

- **Killed caged animals for fun**
- **Supported pepper spraying the eyes of handcuffed peaceful protesters at Highway 55**
- **Supports light rail in the wrong place**
- **Promoted eliminating auto emission testing**
- **Vetoed lawn sprinkler water conservation legislation**

- Illegally spent state money for his excessive personal security
- Spent more than $1.6 billion in tax rebates. Now Minnesota has to raise taxes

Expanded Cast of Characters

Charles Balck, Ramsey County Assistant Attorney who communicated with me about this matter and refused to tell me when, how or who made the decision to send the complaints to Anoka County.

Dean Barkley, Ventura Campaign Committee Chairman. Dean Barkley was the mastermind of the election bribe and fix of the ensuing investigation. At one time he was chairman of the Reform Party (now the Independence Party) and in July 1998, was chairman of the Ventura's campaign committee.

Barkley is no amateur at election laws. An attorney since 1977, he ran for the U.S. House in 1992 and the U.S. Senate in 1994 and 1996. He was a past director of the Common Cause political watchdog group. He is an expert political strategist. He knew he was violating Minnesota law.

Kathleen Blatz, Supreme Court Justice. Blatz made a mistake in the Ole Savior-contested election case by sending it to a lower court when she should have appointed a three judge panel to review it.

Steven Bosacker, Ventura's Chief of Staff. Tim Penny, former Congressman, advised Ventura immediately after his election and recommended Bosacker to head the transition team. Bosacker, from Waseca, Minnesota,

had worked for Penny for 10 years in Washington and
Minnesota in various positions, including chief of staff.
Bosacker was appointed to head Ventura's transition
team on November 9, 1998, and was formally
announced as Ventura's chief of staff on December 15,
1998. Bosacker attended Gustavus Adolphus College
and finished his degree at Metro State. Bosacker
worked for the University of Minnesota as executive
director to the Regents when Ventura obtained him.

Karen Carpenter, Commissioner, Minnesota
Department of Employee Relations. Carpenter was
reappointed by Ventura when he took office. He
commented that she was good at her job. Carpenter
was forced to resign because she would not endorse
Ventura's "conflict of interest" activities, particularly
his participation in the SummerSlam wrestling event
as a referee on August 22, 1999 (*see Leslie Davis lawsuit
filing to prevent Summer Slam conflict of interest and Judge
Gearin ORDER*).

Carpenter's ethics officer, Sandra Hyllengren, had a
meeting with Ventura's staff and sent them a memo
stating that the governor is an employee and subject to
Minnesota Statute 43A.38 that restricts "state
employees" from using their office for personal financial
gain. Hyllengren was also driven out of her office.

Carpenter was a hold-over from former governor
Carlson's administration. In a statement issued by
Ventura, and reported in the *Pioneer Press* on
December 29, 1999, he said she and two other carry-
over commissioners would stay on because they
have "shown extraordinary leadership" in running
their departments.

Julien C. Carter was imported from Jefferson City, Missouri [April 18, 2000] to replace Karen Carpenter as commissioner, Department of Employee Relations. Carpenter was driven from office by Ventura's cronies for refusing to be a pawn and a stooge for the adminis- tration. Carter would fit that bill nicely. He would be a team player at $97,300 per year. His first assignment was to make it clear that Ventura's current and future illegal activities would not be opposed by his office [which is responsible for overseeing conflict of interest matters for the state].

Renee Coffey, Secretary of State staff person who took Bill Dahn's registration for governor in the Reform Party and notarized it. (Jodene Pope was a staff person with Coffey at the time.)

William "Bill" Dahn, bribe victim of Ventura and Barkley. *See Chapter Two.*

Leslie Davis, Author of this book. Earth Protector founder and president (www.EarthProtector.org)

Diane Drewry, Ventura staff person, attorney and girlfriend of Phil Madsen. Madsen was assigned to take Bill Dahn out to eat on July 20 and make sure he stayed in line. I needed to serve papers in a lawsuit on the governor and Metro Legal Services refused to do so because they are Ventura ass kissers. The person I selected to serve Ventura went to the governor's office and I watched her hand the papers to Drewry and also leave one set of papers in a "conspicuous" place as authorized by law. Drewry lied and told the court she never received the papers.

Henry Fieldseth, peace activist who was tortured and arrested during the Ventura supported 1998 Highway 55 raid. More than 600 police arrested 36 people and tortured more than 10 of them so the transportation department could destroy seven houses in the path of a road they wanted to build. The peaceful protesters were occupying the houses to protect them from demolition.

Tom Foley, Former Ramsey County Attorney who hired Gaertner and Wodele. Now a Commissioner with the Metropolitan Airports Commission.

Dick Franson, exposed Ventura as not being a SEAL. Filed first bribery complaint on July 23, 1998.

Doug Friedline, managed the day to day activities of Ventura's 1998 campaign.

On August 25, 1998, Friedline told Ramsey County investigators that he was monitoring the Secretary of State's website when he learned that Bill Dahn had registered for governor in the Reform Party. He told the investigators that he then called the people in the Reform Party. He was assigned the task of finding out about Dahn and he made the arrangements for Ventura and Barkley to meet Dahn at his house on July 19, 1998.

C. Lynne Fundingsland, Acting Deputy-Criminal Division, Minneapolis City Attorney's Office. Dick Franson filed a January 1999 complaint alleging that Susan Gaertner violated Minnesota Statute 211B.16 by stalling the investigation of his earlier July complaint.

On January 13, 1999, Theodore Leon, St. Paul deputy city attorney, sent the matter to Fundingsland of the Minneapolis City attorney's office, alleging that there was a conflict of interest between the St. Paul city attorney and the Ramsey County attorney because they work closely together. Leon asked Fundingsland to review the complaint against Gaertner for "investigation and possible charging."

Leon asked Fundingsland to investigate Gaertner for possible violation of 211B.16 for failing to "promptly investigate" the July complaints against Ventura and Barkley. Minn. Stat. 211B.16 states that, "a county attorney who is notified of an alleged violation of this chapter shall *promptly investigate*. If there is a probable cause for instituting a prosecution, the county shall proceed by complaint or present the charge, with whatever evidence has been found, to the grand jury."

Fundingsland's response letter of February 10, 1999 states that, "there is evidence that the Ramsey County attorney's office promptly *initiated* its investigation of the alleged violation."

Fundingsland obfuscates the issue by arbitrarily introducing the word "initiated" yet the statute says nothing about initiating but clearly says "promptly investigate." Gaertner held the case for five months, yet Fundingsland absurdly and incorrectly gets Gaertner off the hook by inserting the word "initiate." Fundingsland fabricated her answer to protect one of her own.

Susan Gaertner, Ramsey County Attorney. Gaertner is the wife of John Wodele, Governor Ventura's communications director.

Gaertner was hired in 1984 by Ramsey County attorney Tom Foley. One year later Foley would hire his boyhood friend John Wodele to do public relations work for him.

Foley vacated his county attorney position in 1994 when he ran for the U.S. Senate. Gaertner ran for Foley's vacated county attorney position and won.

As Ramsey County attorney she appointed John Wodele as her chief of staff, and in 1997 appointed him to a division director position at $90,000 per year. After complaints by county staff that Gaertner and Wodele were having an affair that was affecting the work of the office, the *St. Paul Pioneer Press* newspaper reported the situation. The story appeared in August 1998 and determined that they were having an affair since at least 1997. Wodele resigned his job on September 9, 1998.

Gaertner was running for reelection at the time of Wodele's resignation and, despite the negative publicity, she kept him on her payroll for at least a month to help with her campaign. They disguised Wodele's extended employment beyond his resignation as necessary for a smooth transition of his previous responsibilities. County staff claim that the office was organized in such a way that Wodele could have left at once.

Kathleen Gearin, Ramsey County District Court Judge. Gearin was the judge in the "conflict of interest" case that I brought against Ventura in August 1999 for his participation as a referee in a World Wrestling Federation (WWF) event at the Target Center. I claimed that Ventura was using his position as governor to obtain the wrestling job that would pay him close to a million dollars or more. *See Chapter Ten, page 89.*

Alan Gilbert, Chief Deputy Minnesota Attorney General. Did the research and report on the employment status of Ventura. His January 15, 1999 report confirmed the fact that the governor is a state employee.

Mike Hatch, Minnesota Attorney General supported Gilbert's finding.

Thomas Heffelfinger, current U.S. attorney for Minnesota. His specialty is white collar crime. He was an attorney for Dean Barkley and Jesse Ventura. Former assistant Hennepin County attorney, assistant U.S. attorney and U.S. attorney. Represented former Governor Arne Carlson, his administration and the Minnesota House Republican caucus.

Heffelfinger was retained to obtain an affidavit from James Kane that would support the false stories told by Ventura/Barkley about their bribery activities in July 1998. At the time Heffelfinger took the affidavit he was Ventura and Barkley's attorney.

Heffelfinger said he acquired the services of James Molnar to assist him in taking Kane's affidavit. Molnar is a private investigator and notary, who worked for Heffelfinger as needed. Molnar and Heffelfinger met Kane in a restaurant in Stillwater, Minnesota where Heffelfinger directed Molnar to hand-write Kane's six page affidavit and notarize it.

On December 28, 1998, Heffelfinger sent Kane's affidavit to Anoka County Prosecutor James Weber who was reviewing the bribery case for Ramsey County.

Weber used information that he could have only gotten from Kane's false affidavit to make his December 31, 1998 findings in the Ventura/Barkley case. Weber's findings stated that, "sufficient probable cause does not exist to charge a criminal offense, no criminal complaint will be issued in this case and no presentation will be made to a grand jury." Weber closed the case and sent the file back to Ramsey County. One month later he was appointed by Ventura to the Commission on Judicial Selection. The Commission screens judicial candidates and makes recommendations to the governor for District Court judgeship and Workers' Compensation Court of Appeals vacancies.

Jay Heffern, Minneapolis City Attorney. Refused to prosecute Ventura on the conflict of interest misdemeanor complaint I filed. Heffern claimed that his staff could not conclude that the governor is a state employee. The state ethics officer, the state attorney general and the state law defines Ventura as an employee, yet Heffern claimed that he couldn't come to that conclusion.

Dennis Hoff, Ramsey County investigator with McNiff

Mavis Huddle, Ventura's campaign secretary. She told Ventura about Dahn calling the campaign party office numerous times. Ventura told Hoff that Huddle told him about Dahn filing for governor.

Sandra Hyllengren, Former Ethics Officer with the Minnesota Department of Employee Relations. She was asked by Ventura chief of staff Bosacker for a determination of the governor's employee status and told them in an August 2, 1999 memo, that the governor is an employee and subject to Minnesota Statute 43A.38, regarding conflict of interest for State employees. For her actions she was driven out of her job along with her boss, Karen Carpenter, commissioner of employee relations. Julien Carter was imported from Jefferson City, Missouri to help fix the previous allegations against Ventura's conflict of interest matters and to obfuscate his ongoing illegal activities. Carter could be considered little more than a high paid prevaricator.

James Kane, Bill Dahn's cousin and lieutenant governor candidate. On August 14, 1998, Kane denied a request by Ramsey County investigators to appear for an interview about the bribery complaints.

In November Barkley told Kane that Dahn was acting up, and threatening to make trouble because his house wasn't getting fixed. Barkley told Kane that if he didn't help he could be found guilty of taking the bribe to withdraw his candidacy. Barkley knew that the case would be going to Anoka County and he wanted to provide prosecutor Weber with an affidavit that would support the lies so he could make his finding of no probable cause.

Thomas Heffelfinger arranged for Kane to give him his affidavit on November 24, 1998 in a Stillwater, Minnesota restaurant. Heffelfinger was accompanied by James Molnar, a private investigator and notary public. Molnar recorded the six page, hand-written sworn affidavit that supported the lies Barkley laid out for him.

Amy Klobuchar, Hennepin County Attorney. I filed a misdemeanor complaint with her alleging that Ventura violated state conflict of interest law by referring a wrestling event on August 22, 1999. Klobuchar, after a lengthy and self-serving letter, advised me that her office handles felony matters and my complaint should go to the Minneapolis city attorney.

Theodore D. Leon, St. Paul Deputy City Attorney acted for city attorney Clayton Robinson. Leon sent Dick Franson's January 1999 complaint about Gaertner stalling the bribery investigation to Minneapolis acting deputy attorney C. Lynne Fundingsland. Leon stated that his office had a conflict of interest in this matter because his office often works with Gaertner's office. Fundingsland made an incorrect decision in favor of Gaertner.

Phil Madsen, Ventura operative and boyfriend of Diane Drewry. Madsen was assigned to babysit Bill Dahn on July 20, 1998 to make sure he was going to follow through on withdrawing his candidacy on July 21, 1998.

Joe Mansky, Elections Officer with Secretary of State in 1998. He confirmed that his office didn't advise Dahn what to do, they just explain the rules to the candidates. He, Renee Coffey and Jodene Pope were in the office during the July 1998 registration period and they all confirm that Dahn was not misled. Why would they?

Gerald McNiff, Ramsey County investigator with Hoff

James Molnar, Private investigator retained by Heffelfinger to take Kane's affidavit in a Stillwater restaurant. Molnar had done work for Heffelfinger in the past. Molnar notarized Kane's affidavit. When I contacted Molnar to talk about this he told me to contact Heffelfinger.

Tim Penny, a former Congressman from Southern Minnesota. Ventura was advised to call Penny for help in assembling his administration. Penny recommended Steven Bosacker to head the transition team. Bosacker had worked for Penny when he was in Congress. Ventura appointed Bosacker to head the transition team and on December 15, 1998 named him as his chief of staff. Prior to joining Ventura's team, Bosacker worked for the University of Minnesota.

Jodene Pope, Minnesota Secretary of State staff person in July 1998 when the Dahn registration took place. (Renee Coffey was also a staff person.)

Bill Salisbury, former U.S. Navy SEAL commander

Ole Savior, Candidate for Governor 1998

Joe Soucheray, KSTP-AM radio announcer. Soucheray interviewed Ventura on July 22, 1998, the day after Barkley paid $600 to the Secretary of State for Dahn to register as a Republican. In the transcript Soucheray says to Ventura, "You bought the guy" (Dahn) and Ventura responds, "And the point is so what if we did that? What's the big deal about it?"

Tony Trimble, Attorney for Minnesota Republican Party

Jesse Ventura, Governor of Minnesota

Phil Villaume, Attorney for Jesse Ventura and Dean Barkley. Brother of Dean Barkley's wife. Acted as Dahn's attorney when he canceled a court appearance on a speeding ticket in Washington County. Villiaume told Thomas Heffilfinger to send James Kane's affidavit to Anoka County Prosecutor Weber on December 28, 1998. How did Villaume know that Heffelfinger had such an affidavit? How did Villaume know that Weber of Anoka County had the case from Ramsey County? When Franson, the Republicans and Ole Savior inquired about the status of the case they were told that it was an ongoing investigation and no information could be given out. How did Villaume know so much of what was going on?

Charlie Weaver, currently Minnesota Commissioner of Public Safety. Former Anoka County prosecutor, former state legislator and long-time friend of James Weber, who made the findings in the Ventura/Barkley bribery case. Weaver lost the November 1998 election for attorney general to Mike Hatch. After the election, Barkley picked Weaver for a Ventura advisory committee. What did Barkley want with the unemployed Weaver? Weaver was in debt from his campaign run for attorney general. Weaver rejected a position he was offered...he wanted to be commissioner of public safety. The top cop. The biggest paycheck Weaver ever received in his life. He got it.

James Weber, Anoka County, Chief Criminal Prosecutor. Weber acknowledged receipt of the case from Ramsey County on December 23, 1998. He received Kane's affidavit by fax from Heffelfinger on December 28, 1998. How did Heffelfinger know Weber had the case? Villaume told him.

John Wodele, Ventura Communications Director and husband of Ramsey County Attorney Susan Gaertner. (See Chapter Eight, page 64)

Chronology

<u>1998</u>

1/26: Ventura announces he will run for governor.

7/14: Dahn pays a $600 non-refundable fee to register to run for governor in the Reform Party.

7/15: Friedline learns about Dahn's Reform Party registration. Alerts Barkley and others.

7/16: Friedline assigned to learn about Dahn and report back.

7/17: Friedline arranges a July 19, 1998 meeting for Ventura and Barkley at Dahn's house.

7/19: Ventura and Barkley go to Dahn's house to bribe him to withdraw from the Reform Party so Ventura can keep his radio show and eliminate his competition in the September primary.

7/20: Madsen assigned to watch Dahn and make sure he stays in line.

7/21: Ventura registers to run for governor at 2:00 p.m.

7/21: Dahn withdraws from the Reform Party after 3:00 p.m., registers as a Republican and Barkley pays his new $600 registration fee.

7/21: Dick Franson knocks Ventura off the air by threatening KFAN radio that he would complain to the FCC if other candidates were denied equal time.

7/21: 6:00 p.m., KFAN radio announces that Ventura is off the air.

7/22: Ventura interviews with radio talk show host Joe Soucheray and admits buying off Dahn.

7/22: *Star Tribune* reports Dahn withdraws from the Reform Party, registers as a Republican.

7/22: *St. Paul Pioneer Press* reports that Barkley paid $600 for Dahn to register as a Republican.

7/23: Franson files bribery complaint against Barkley with Ramsey County attorney.

7/24: Minnesota Republican Party files a bribery complaint similar to Franson's.

7/24: *Star Tribune* reports Franson's complaint against Barkley.

7/25: *St. Paul Pioneer Press* reports the complaints.

8/06: Barkley is interviewed and tape recorded by Ramsey County investigators.

8/14: Dahn and Kane notify investigators that they will not consent to be interviewed.

8/25: Friedline interviewed and tape recorded by Ramsey County investigators.

9/03: Ventura interviewed and tape recorded by Ramsey County investigators.

9/03: Memo of Barkley working to get Dahn's house fixed as part of the bribe.

9/09: Wodele resigns his $90,000 job with Ramsey County.

9/15: Ramsey County investigators complete the bribery investigation and file report.

9/15: Ventura, with no opposition, wins Reform Party primary election.

10/09: Wodele's last day of employment at Ramsey County.

10/20: Barkley gets letter about Dahn from Interior Finish Group.

11/03: Ventura wins election for governor.

11/03: Susan Gaertner wins re-election as Ramsey County attorney.

11/04: Ole Savior visits investigator Hoff and Hoff adds a meaningless memo to the file.

11/10: Ole Savior files a contested election lawsuit. A comedy of errors ensues.

11/09: Bosacker is appointed chief of staff for Ventura's transition team.

11/12: Wodele calls Bosacker and tells him that he is available to serve Ventura.

11/17: Charlie Weaver appointed to Ventura's transition advisory committee.

11/24: Heffelfinger takes affidavit from James Kane, Dahn running mate.

11/24: Barkley gets fax about Dahn from Ramsey Action Programs.

12/07: Ventura takes Weaver with him to kill caged pheasants at a game farm.

12/15: Barkley gets letter about Dahn from the Department of Children, Families & Learning.

12/15: Bosacker is named Ventura's chief of staff.

12/17: Gaertner cites conflict of interest and sends the complaints to Anoka County.

12/20: Ventura supports Highway 55 raid where people were handcuffed and tortured.

12/28: Heffelfinger sends Kane's affidavit to James Weber in Anoka County.

12/28: Wodele is named Ventura's communications director.

12/31: Weber dismisses the bribery complaints.

1999

1/02: Weaver is appointed Commissioner, Department of Public Safety.

1/04: Ventura inauguration.

1/06: Barkley is appointed Director of Minnesota Planning.

1/07: Franson files a complaint, alleging that Gaertner stalled complaint outcome.

1/13: St. Paul city attorney cites conflict of interest; sends Franson complaint to Minneapolis.

2/04: Weber appointed to Governor's Commission on Judicial Selection.

2/04: Villaume appointed to Governor's Commission on Judicial Selection.

2/10: Minneapolis City Attorney Fundingsland finds Gaertner did not stall the outcome of the 161 day-old investigation.

2/17: St. Paul city attorney advises Franson of Minneapolis decision and closes file.

8/02: Minnesota Ethics Officer Sandra Hyllengren opines [August 2, 1999] that Ventura is an employee and is subject to state conflict of interest laws.

8/18: Common Cause files a conflict complaint with the Department of Employee Relations.

8/18: Davis files lawsuit and restraining order request to prevent Ventura wrestling referee gig.

8/20: Judge Kathleen Gearin dismisses Davis' lawsuit for his lack of 'standing.'

8/22: Ventura referees WWF wrestling event at Target Center.

8/26: Davis files complaint with Hennepin County Attorney Klobuchar.

8/27: Klobuchar rejects Davis' misdemeanor complaint because the county only handles felony matters.

2000

2/09: Ethics Officer Hyllengren resigns over the effects of her August 2, 1999 memo that stated that Ventura is an employee and subject to state conflict of interest laws.

11/30: Davis files misdemeanor complaint against Ventura for his wrestling referee conflict of interest with Minneapolis city attorney, Jay Heffern.

2001

01/29: Heffern takes two months to reject Davis, claiming that his staff cannot prove beyond a reasonable doubt that the governor is an employee of the state.

ORDER A BOOK FOR A FRIEND

Book	$12.95
Postage and Handling	$3.05
	$16.00

Shipped within 7 days of receipt of your check.

SEND TO: _____

_____

_____

phone and/or email (optional) _____

SEND TO: _____

_____

_____

phone and/or email (optional) _____

Number of books at $12.95 = _____

Postage and handling $3.05 = _____

Grand total = _____

Please send your check and order form to:

> Tell The Truth Books, Inc.
> P.O. Box 11688
> Minneapolis, MN 55411

Please remember to enclose your check.

ORDER A BOOK FOR A FRIEND

Book	$12.95
Postage and Handling	$3.05
	$16.00

Shipped within 7 days of receipt of your check.

SEND TO: _____

_____

_____

phone and/or email (optional) _____

SEND TO: _____

_____

_____

phone and/or email (optional) _____

Number of books at $12.95 = _____

Postage and handling $3.05 = _____

Grand total = _____

Please send your check and order form to:

Tell The Truth Books, Inc.
P.O. Box 11688
Minneapolis, MN 55411

Please remember to enclose your check.